Crazy-makers and I

Handling Passive-Aggressive People

Monica A. Frank, Ph.D.

Excel At Life, LLC

Crazy-makers and Mean People: Handling Passive-Aggressive People

All rights reserved.

www.ExcelAtLife.com

Contents

Chapter 1

Crazy-makers: Passive-aggressive People

I'm sure you've dealt with individuals who have caused you to be so frustrated that afterwards you scratch your head asking "Am I crazy?" Most likely you just had an encounter with a passive-aggressive person. Such encounters may include sarcasm, shifting blame, saying one thing while meaning another to name a few. For instance, I used to know a co-worker who was very skilled at giving back-handed compliments such as "You look great! You must be doing something different" as well as sarcasm disguised as a compliment "Oh, I hear you've managed to pull off another miracle." The problem with these kinds of comments is that if you try to confront them about the insult, you will be accused of not understanding, "I didn't mean it that way" or of misinterpreting, "You must have a problem to think that. I was just trying to compliment you. Sorry I didn't word it right to suit you." As a result, you end up looking like the bad guy, feeling frustrated, and asking yourself, "Am I crazy?" And the other person walks away blameless.

What is Passive-aggressive Behavior?

Passive-aggressive communication seeks to control the emotions of others and thereby, control their behavior. Typically, this communication style seeks to express anger in an indirect manner. By doing so the individual is able to deny all responsibility for the anger yet they score a direct hit on their target. A common example is criticizing as if you are concerned, "You've put on so much weight! You might get diabetes or heart disease if you don't take it easy with the sweets." Certainly, in the right context this could actually be an expression of concern. However, the right context doesn't include making such a statement in front of others just as the individual is taking a bite of dessert. In this instance, if the comment is confronted, the person will often deny responsibility by stating something like, "I'm just concerned about you. Wow, are you sensitive!"

The best way to recognize passive-aggressive behavior is by analyzing the process and purpose of the behavior. Typically, as the purpose is to control and/or deflect responsibility for anger, the passive-aggressive behavior causes frustration or anger in the recipient and will escalate conflict unless the recipient handles it passively by swallowing, ignoring, or discounting their anger. Yet, if the purpose is to escalate conflict, the passive-aggressive behavior is calculated to cause the recipient to act unreasonably.

For example, a father conveys the subtle message of "I don't think you're capable" by taking on a task to do it right, "Here, let me help you cut that out" as he takes over the child's school project. When the child states "I can do it myself" the father keeps working on the project "I know you can. I'm just helping. Now doesn't that look better?" If the child should protest angrily, "You don't think I can do it right!" the father might respond "Of course I do. I was just helping. You are so ungrateful!"

In this situation, the father has escalated the situation to cause the child to become angry and then to criticize the child for being angry. This teaches the child that her emotions are unacceptable as well as that her father doesn't believe she is capable. Over time the child learns to not trust her own perceptions of reality.

Another common example may be when a couple are trying to make a simple decision such as where to go for dinner. The wife says, "I don't care" but then pouts when her husband decides. When her husband asks her what is wrong she responds "You know I don't like Chinese." Later on in a completely unrelated situation, she may even take this a step further "You make all the decisions and don't take my preferences into account!" This can become even more ugly if the wife should accuse the husband of deliberately mistreating her "You do whatever you want. You don't care about my feelings!"

This example shows how a simple situation can escalate to include many different situations. The passive-aggressive wife can angrily attack her husband while blaming him for the attack. He becomes confused and angry "You're crazy!" which allows his wife to prove her point "See how you treat me? Calling me names and putting me down!"

Categories of Passive-Aggressive People

Although passive-aggressive behavior is generally hurtful to the recipient, the intention is not always for the purpose of hurting the other person. Therefore, whether the intention to hurt is present can categorize the type of passive-aggressive person.

Malicious type

Some passive-aggressive people deliberately attempt to cause the other person to become angry so as to displace their own feelings of anger onto the recipient. In this situation, if a man has a bad day at work he can create an argument at home in a passive-aggressive manner and then take his anger out on his wife. For instance, he comes home, glances around and asks "What have you been doing today?" When his wife becomes defensive "Are you saying that I'm lazy?" he responds with "You are really over-reacting! I was only curious about what you did today. You are so sensitive and I can't even talk to you!"

This type of person could be labeled an aggressive passive-aggressive in that the purpose is to create anger or to try to control someone else. "You should really try to treat your mother better after all the sacrifices I've made for you. You're so selfish" is an example of trying to control behavior. By negatively labeling a behavior, they hope to control the person's responses. The malicious type is reinforced whenever they can successfully control the other person or when they can escalate conflict while remaining seemingly innocent.

Unintentionally hurtful type

Another type of passive-aggressive person we could label as the passive passive-aggressive. Typically, they are trying not to hurt the other person but in the process may unintentionally cause frustration or irritation. This person also is trying to control the other person such as trying to control the other person's emotions. They don't want the other person to feel bad so they will try to refrain from any communication that may seem negative. However, their feelings may be readable at a nonverbal level. Unfortunately, the other person may not read the feelings accurately.

For instance, a girlfriend is hoping that her boyfriend will pick up on her hints about wanting to get engaged but doesn't express her wishes; she becomes irritated with him and when he picks up on the nonverbal frustration and asks if anything is wrong, she says, "No." However, he becomes less certain about their relationship due to this passive-aggressive interaction.

Another example is a man who is disappointed that his wife passed up a job opportunity but doesn't want to tell her how he feels because he doesn't want to hurt her feelings. However, his disappointment leads to him unknowingly being less affectionate causing his wife to believe that he is less attracted to her.

Types of Passive-aggressive Behavior

As you see from some of the previous examples, passive-aggressive behavior is manifested in many ways. Although the bottom line in identifying the behavior is that it succeeds in indirectly expressing anger; the passive-aggressive individual does not have to take responsibility for the controlling behavior and angry message. However, we can divide the behaviors into several common categories as described below. Obviously, you will see that these behaviors often overlap so more than one may occur in a situation.

Denial

This type of passive-aggressive behavior occurs when the individual appears to be distressed, frustrated, bored, confused, or any number of emotions but when questioned refuses to admit to the feeling. They may outright deny or they may avoid by ignoring, working, or deflecting with humor. However, the behavior has the outcome of frustrating the recipient because they are unable to confront and resolve the problem. Thus, this individual is able to control the other by not engaging in conflict resolution when an obvious problem has occurred.

Blaming

The skilled passive-aggressive blamer can rephrase almost any comment to make it appear the recipient's fault. "You should have known!" or "You're too sensitive!" are common methods of blaming the victim. Sometimes it can be so extreme as to border on the ridiculous if it wasn't so hurtful; for example, "You know I'm a grouch before dinner. I wouldn't have yelled at you if you wouldn't have asked me a question." This person deflects all attempts to communicate about problems by blaming the other person.

Revenge-Seeking

This behavior is calculated to try to hurt the other person without taking responsibility. An example of this is described above with the "back-handed compliment." The individual somehow is threatened by the other, whether real or imagined, and seeks revenge in an underhanded manner. By doing so, they can claim ignorance if confronted such as "I had no idea you would take it that way" or resort to blaming "You must be imagining that. I would never do anything to hurt you."

Controlling

This behavior seeks to control the individual in an indirect manner. For instance, a man who emotionally abuses his partner says "No one could ever love you the way I do" with the intended result being insecurity in the woman so that she won't leave him. Another example is parents telling their adult children that they should respect or love them because they are their parents thus trying to control their behavior. Love and respect is something that occurs due to the underlying relationship not because of a demand.

Guilting

This behavior controls through using guilt either directly or indirectly to control the other. An indirect form of guilt may be "Don't worry about me...I'll be okay" followed by a sigh. A more direct form may be describing all the efforts made on your behalf followed by an expectation "I've only cleaned the house today, taken the kids to their activities, checked on your mom. Taking me out to dinner isn't too much to ask, is it?"

Sarcastic

Many of the examples above contain sarcasm probably because it tends to be a favorite of mine. Sarcastic passive-aggressive comments are the ultimate indirect form of aggression because they are calculated to avoid responsibility such as "You know I was just kidding." Yet, they have the impact of controlling the other person's emotions and potentially their thinking and behavior.

Back-stabbing

This behavior often uses techniques such as hitting below the belt by using previously confided or sensitive information against the person or by communicating through someone else but with plausible deniability. This individual may even resort to showing artificial concern as a way of validating their behavior "You know I wouldn't want to hurt you but I'm only saying this because I'm concerned about you."

As you can see with the examples in this article, many times the actual words that the passive-aggressive person uses may seem reasonable or even caring. Therefore, to determine passive-aggressive behavior, the context, the relationship, previous experiences with the individual, and the non-verbal communication needs to be considered. However, without even considering all of these factors, you usually know that you are the recipient of passive-aggressive behavior by your own emotional reaction. If you feel frustrated, deflated, or crazy as a result of an interaction, it probably was passive-aggressive.

How Do You Handle Passive-Aggressive People?

This needs to be the subject of a separate article. In fact, what I would like to do is to use some real-life examples that people submit and discuss them in detail in another article. So, if you have an example, please submit it on the form below by describing the situation in detail, your relationship with the person, and the specifics of what was said and how it was said. Examples are included in this ebook.

Although each situation may vary, there are some basic steps you can take with passive-aggressive behavior.

Identify the reward

Determine what the passive-aggressive person achieves by engaging in the behavior. Do they get something they want? Do they make you feel bad? Do they discharge their anger on to you so they can feel better? Do they escalate conflict so they can make you look bad?

Refuse to provide the reward

If you refuse to provide the reward, they are no longer in control of the interaction which tends to cause the situation to backfire on them. For instance, when the co-worker I described earlier would give me a back-handed compliment I would effusively respond "Oh, that's so nice of you to say that! I really appreciate it!" as if it were a true compliment. This would have the effect of making her believe that she had not accomplished her purpose (which she hadn't anyway because I was thinking "How silly of a grown adult to act this way") which tended to reduce the behavior because she was getting her reward of feeling better at my expense.

If you determine that the individual is trying to escalate conflict, then you want to become even more calm almost to an extreme. The more calm you become, the more apparent and ridiculous their behavior will appear. Plus, you are not allowing them to get the reward of freely discharging their anger on to you. What I mean is that if you allow the situation to escalate, they will then engage in a full battle while blaming you for "starting" the argument.

Indirectly confront

Obviously, as I described above, if you directly confront the passive-aggressive person is likely to turn it against you. But if you confront with "I" statements instead of "you" statements and remain very calm you may be able to reduce the behavior. Although you are unlikely to get them to admit they were wrong, since they do not like to take responsibility, they are more likely to reduce the behavior if they know they will be confronted every time.

The following example uses the broken-record technique in which you repeatedly make your point of letting them know how you feel when they act in a passive-aggressive manner.

"You need to be careful what you're eating. You're getting fat."

"I feel hurt when you call me fat."

"I'm just saying that because I'm concerned about you."

"But I feel hurt when you call me that."

"You're just too sensitive!"

"That may be, but I'm letting you know that I feel hurt when you call me names." This statement uses the technique of agreeing with them but still using the broken record to make your point.

"You need to just get over it."

"Since I've told you that I feel hurt when you call me names should I assume that you are trying to hurt me when you call me names?" This last line should not be uttered unless the passive-aggressive person persists.

Escalation of Behavior When Setting Limits

When you start changing a behavior pattern in which you've engaged with someone for a period of time, sometimes you may see the behavior get worse. Although sometimes this is because you are still learning and needing more practice, many times it occurs because the person will try to escalate the behavior in order to obtain their reward. It is much different from trying to change a child's temper tantrums. If you have been rewarding the child by trying to quiet her with a piece of candy whenever she has a temper tantrum and then you decided to stop doing that, you will initially see an increase in the temper tantrums. However, if you remain firm and consistent, eventually they will decrease.

It will take time to learn to handle passive-aggressive people, however, it will be well worth the effort. When I'm working with clients frequently it will take a number of tries and adjustments in our approach but if we examine the behavior and the reward process we can usually find a method that can work.

Chapter 2

7 Rules and 8 Methods for Responding to Passive-aggressive People

The most difficult social conflict usually involves passive-aggressive (PA) behavior. The reason it is more distressing than even aggressive behavior is because it causes the recipient to be doubtful of him or her self. When someone is aggressive towards you, their intention is clear and it is easier to make a decision such as "I need to steer clear of this person" or "I need to report this behavior." However, the purpose of passive-aggressive behavior is for the aggressor to avoid responsibility for their actions. PA behavior can easily be denied or blame shifted: "I didn't mean it the way you took it" or "You're being too sensitive" or "You're just trying to get me in trouble."

As a result, PA behavior cannot be addressed in the same way you might handle aggressive behavior. When managing PA people you need to be aware of the underlying purpose of the behavior so that you can respond in a way that prevents them from succeeding at their agenda. The less likely they are to achieve their goal, the more likely you will see a reduction in their behavior.

Rules When Dealing With Passive-aggressive People

The following rules provide some guidelines to managing PA people. As you read these rules it may seem impossible to develop an appropriate response on the spur of the moment when confronted with PA behavior because there are so many things to consider. However, much of the time certain people in your life probably engage in repeated PA behavior which gives you the opportunity to prepare in advance. Once you have practiced the skills in predictable situations, you will be better able to manage the less predictable ones.

Rule 1. Identify type of PA behavior

The first step when confronted with PA behavior is to determine whether it is malicious or self-protective or unintentional. By knowing the type of PA behavior, you will be able to develop a better response to help you achieve your goal.

Unintentional. Unintentional PA behavior is the easiest to handle because you can just ignore the behavior if it is not that important. Or, if it is bothersome, you can let the other person know how you feel. When the PA behavior is unintentional, directly expressing yourself is more likely to result in a behavior change than when the behavior is self-protective or malicious. For example, a person slams a door when angry. If this behavior is unintentional and you express how you feel, the person might change their behavior. "I know you are angry, but I would appreciate it if you don't slam the door."

Self-protective. Self-protective PA behavior may or may not be changeable based on the person's need for the protection and their level of denial. People have a variety of needs for protection such as protecting their self-concept or protecting their job or protecting their personal interests. For instance, a person who wants to believe they are acting in your best interest, when instead, they are being hurtful may be protecting their self-image. Directly confronting them is likely to cause them to blame you and not obtain the result you want:

"I think you need to be more careful about what you eat."

"Please don't criticize me."

"I'm not criticizing. I'm just concerned about your health."

However, by recognizing the purpose of their behavior, you may be able to address it more effectively, "I know you care about me, but when you tell me about what I should and shouldn't eat, I feel as if you are criticizing me rather than helping."

Malicious. A malicious person doesn't care about you and only desires to hurt you in such a way so as to avoid any responsibility for their behavior. In other words, they want to look blameless while driving the knife into your gut. With such people any response can potentially escalate the situation in their favor. Your response needs to be well thought out and should be based upon how they affect your life. For instance, if it is a malicious co-worker, your response may need to be focused on how others perceive the situation and damage control. Yet, you need to consider your response carefully to prevent the malicious person from turning co-workers or managers against you. If your response escalates the situation, you may look like the bad guy and be the recipient of negative consequences rather than the malicious aggressor.

Rule 2. Recognize when you need to address your thinking or behavior.

Over-reaction. Other people's behavior may not always be PA just because it feels hurtful. Be sure to have insight into yourself and recognize when you might be over-reacting to people's comments.

Even if you are uncertain about whether you are over-reacting, the nice thing about most of the responses to PA behavior is that the responses can be framed in such a way that if the behavior is not PA, your response can still be an appropriate response. For example, someone makes a joke and you're not sure if it is just an innocent joke or whether they are laughing at you. Calmly asking, "Are you talking about me?" can clarify the situation without unduly confronting the person. However, if they are joking about you, your statement would be perceived as a confrontation and the person may be less likely to the do the same again.

Demands. Recognize when you may have unreasonable demands or expectations. Sometimes we may view others as PA when they don't meet our expectations. For instance, you ask your boss for some help and she assigns a co-worker who doesn't complete the work the way you would. You think, "She's just mad that she has to help me." In this case, the person could be PA but it also could be your expectations. You need to be able to clearly define when you are being unreasonable.

However, as I stated before, your response can be the same whether the person is PA or not because either way you do not want to accuse the person of deliberately doing the job wrong. If the person is PA then she could blame you, complain to the boss, and get away with not doing the work. And if she's not PA then you would look unreasonable. Assertive directions in this situation would be best: "I realize you don't do this all the time. Could you do it this way for me?"

When you are passive-aggressive. Recognize when you may be passive-aggressive because you may need to stop your PA behavior to address the other person's PA behavior. For example, if you are giving your spouse the silent treatment in reaction to PA behavior, you may need to change your response before you can request a change from your spouse.

Rule 3. Determine the person's reward.

One of the best ways to know how to respond to a PA person is to determine the reward for their behavior. In the situation with the co-worker not doing the job right, the reward to escalating conflict and your frustration is to not have to do the job at all.

There is always some sort of reward to PA behavior. Do they get their way? Are they able to feel better due to transferring their anger, anxiety, stress onto you? Do they get others' approval? Do they satisfy a need to be mean without having to be responsible? These are some of the rewards. Sometimes the rewards may be more tangible such as making you look bad so they can get a promotion at work.

Once you determine the reward, then you are able to develop a response that is based upon not allowing the PA person to get the reward. When you consider your response, you need to think about whether it contributes to obtaining the reward or whether it prevents the reward to the PA person.

Rule 4. Choose your goal.

Before you respond to a person's PA behavior you need to choose the outcome that you want and to determine whether this goal is achievable.

Do you want to change the person's behavior? Do you want to derail the PA behavior by stopping the person from being rewarded? Do you want to manage the fall-out and the perception of others? In many situations your goal is to get out of their trap and to put them in a box where their only response is to stop being PA or to have to be responsible for their behavior (which often stops the PA behavior).

If you want to change the behavior, you also need to determine if the outcome is worth the effort. By asking yourself these questions, you can determine what your goal is so that your response will be based upon how to achieve that goal.

Rule 5. Always remain calm.

In this type of situation, the calm person is more likely to succeed. The passive-aggressive person wants to attribute blame and it is easiest to blame someone when they are out-of-control. You need to remain calm no matter what your goal and chosen response. Otherwise, you will fall into the PA trap and be blamed.

Obviously, many PA people are very skilled at pushing the sensitive buttons of their victim especially if they know you well. As a result, it can be very difficult to remain calm when confronted with their PA accusations. If you anticipate this may be true for you, then practice either through role-playing with someone, imagining the situation in your mind, or in front of a mirror. Imagine the PA behavior and practice remaining calm.

Rule 6. Choose your words carefully

Words are powerful. The words you choose can either de-escalate a situation, resolve the problem, or make the other person look like the bad guy instead of you. Choosing your words may take some practice. This is where role-playing or practicing the words in your head can be helpful. Think about how the PA person might respond to the different words that you use.

Although many different word choices can be used, the "one-down" and the "did I understand you" approaches can be particularly effective when dealing with PA people.

One-down approach. I call this the "Columbo" approach from an old TV series of a detective whose apparent appearance as a bumbling fool caught the criminals off-guard. He made statements such as "Maybe I'm wrong" or "I don't know but..." while scratching his head in confusion.

The one-down approach involves leaving room for disagreement which in the case of a PA person may require them to take a stance. For instance, saying "Maybe I'm wrong, but it seems to me that you are angry" either gets a response of "No, I'm not" or an explanation. However, the "no, I'm not" is usually less accusatory when responding to the one-down approach than it would be if confronted directly. This allows you to then completely ignore the PA message, "Oh, okay, I guess I was wrong" whereas a "No, I'm not!" to a "You're angry!" might lead to an escalation.

Keep in mind that the PA person wants to deliver a message without having to be responsible for it. The one-down approach can prevent the delivery of the message so that the PA person is not rewarded for the behavior.

Did I understand you? approach. I think of this as the Miss Manners approach based on the etiquette advice columnist. She has such a delightful approach to insults or apparent insults while remaining polite. Basically, she advises making a statement expressed with a confused tone such as "Did I hear you correctly? Did you just make a comment about my weight?" or "I must have misunderstood you. I thought you just ask a very personal question." Similar to the one-down approach, this requires the PA person to take a stand and either back off from the original statement or take responsibility for it. If they actually take responsibility for it, you then have the opportunity for a more direct confrontation.

Rule 7. Be assertive.

When you are dealing with a PA person and you decide to confront the behavior directly, being assertive is the best approach. Assertion is expressing how you feel without being derogatory. Although verbal aggression is also a way to confront the behavior and to express yourself, you are more likely to escalate the situation and lose the battle. Adhering to the following components of assertion create a greater likelihood of a satisfactory outcome.

Direct. When being assertive, a direct and to the point approach is best. Say what you need to say as concisely as possible. Being concise doesn't always mean being brief because it depends upon the situation. Factually describing what occurred may require a detailed explanation. However, stay with the facts of the present situation and only describe what is necessary to make your point.

Being direct also means direct contact. Face-to-face interaction is best when confronting someone as it allows you the most information regarding the other person's response. For instance, if you are confronting by phone you don't know if the other person is rolling his eyes and shaking his head during the conversation. People are more likely to be responsive during direct communication.

"I" statements. Using a "you" approach is experienced as aggressive and the other person is likely to become defensive. In the case of a PA person, they are more likely to achieve their agenda with a "you" focus because they can easily deny your statement. "You are hurting my feelings" may get a response such as "No, I'm not, you're just too sensitive" which leads into a discussion of how sensitive you are. Although "I feel hurt when you say that" can also get the response "You're too sensitive" it provides more of an opportunity to stay on topic: "Maybe that's true but I still feel hurt when you say that. Please don't do it again."

Statement of fact. Frequently, when people confront PA behavior, they make an interpretation: "You are deliberately hurting my feelings." The word "deliberately" in this statement makes it an interpretation. With PA people an interpretation provides them with the ammunition they desire because it is easy for them to deny and then accuse you of being wrong and hurtful. "How dare you accuse me of deliberately trying to hurt you! What kind of person do you think I am?"

When confronting, stick to the facts. This means to describe exactly what occurred without providing a reason. Instead of "You're trying to do this task wrong so that I will take over and you won't have to do it" try "Be sure to do the job the correct way or you might have to do it over again."

Tone of voice. Your tone should always be firm and sincere. PA people are masters of sarcasm and will pick up on any hint of insincerity. It is easier to be sincere when you make statements of fact using "I" statements and follow the other rules of managing PA people such as choosing your goal and choosing your word choice.

Eye contact. Maintaining good eye contact when assertively confronting someone helps to show sincerity and intention. Often people may choose the right words but their non-verbal expressions may negate their intention. For instance, saying "Don't do that again" while looking at the floor won't be as effective as looking directly at the person.

Facial expression. Always maintain a neutral to pleasant facial expression. Again, using the right word choice won't be as effective if you have an angry expression. The more that you are able to stay calm (Rule 5), the more easily you will be able to maintain an appropriate facial expression. If you look angry, the PA person will be able to make accusations and escalate the situation. Remember, the largest part of communication is non-verbal.

To help a client of mine learn the skills of social interaction, we studied YouTube videos of President Bill Clinton who I consider a master at assertive communication being interviewed by confrontational people such as Bill O'Reilly. Very clearly, President Clinton used this method of maintaining a positive facial expression. In fact, it appeared that the more he was confronted, the more pleasant his expression became. Compare this to O'Reilly confronting President Obama prior to the 2014 Super Bowl. Although President Obama is also very skilled at responding to confrontation, his micro-expressions appear to convey distaste or defensiveness whereas President Clinton always appears to genuinely like the interviewer as well as be interested in having the discussion.

Open stance. You also express yourself through the position of your body. If your arms are crossed you will appear more defensive. If you are pointing at the other person you will seem to be aggressive. Again, even though you use the right words, you may express a different message through your posture. The best body position is to have an open stance which means not having your arms or legs crossed and to have your arms relaxed at your sides.

Methods to Use With Passive-aggressive People

Once you have the rules for managing PA people firmly in mind and feel comfortable with being able to use these rules in your interactions with PA people, the following methods can provide further direction. These methods may be used individually or in combination. Sometimes you may try one and if that doesn't work follow with another one. The methods are in no particular order and should be used based upon your goal and what you have determined previously regarding the PA person's intent and reward.

Method 1. Active listening technique

I like this technique because it is generally an effective method of communication, and yet, if someone is being PA it becomes an indirect way of confronting the person about the PA communication. As such, it is likely to result in a reduction of the PA behavior.

This method is to listen intently to the other person, show an interest in what they are saying, and respond once they are finished. When you respond, restate their comments: "So, I understand that you are saying...Is that correct?" For example, "So, I understand that you are saying I'm fat because I eat too many snack foods. Is that correct?" Notice that you are just restating what was said but doing it in such a way that requires the PA person to take responsibility for their statement. As I've said previously, this is the very thing the PA person doesn't want to do so you are likely to see a reduction in the PA behavior over time if you continue to make them responsible for their statements.

In addition, the active listening technique reduces acting on assumptions. If you are wrong about the statement being PA, this technique allows you to obtain clarification prior to any further action.

Finally, this method allows you to confront them with feelings once you have clarified their intent: "I feel hurt that you feel it is necessary to say that as if I am not aware of the problem. It comes across as criticism."

Method 2. Laugh and agree technique

The laugh and agree technique works well with sarcasm because it ignores the sarcasm. For example, the PA co-worker sarcastically criticizes you for arriving late to work, "Must be nice to sleep in" and you respond "Yeah, it is" completely negates the sarcastic criticism.

A "thank you" can do the same thing to sarcastic or backhanded insults. "You look interested for a change." Saying "thank you" ignores the insult which is frustrating for the PA person who wants to convey a message without taking responsibility for the message.

Method 3. Questioning technique

The questioning technique makes the PA person have to justify and support their statement. PA people don't want to explain because, again, it forces them to take responsibility for their statements. When you use the questioning technique, it needs to be done innocently with genuine interest: "Oh, why do you say that?"

Method 4. The broken record technique

The broken record technique is a method of assertion that can be used to confront behavior. For those of you too young to remember broken records, this technique refers to when a record (a vinyl album used to play music prior to CDs, MP3 players, and smartphones) was scratched, it might keep playing the same phrase over and over.

The purpose of this technique is to not get drawn back into the argument. Once you have responded, continue to repeat your main points no matter how the person tries to deflect, accuse, or otherwise distort the situation.

"I told you that was hurtful. Please don't say it again."

"You're too sensitive."

"I said it was hurtful. Don't say it again."

"I didn't mean it that way."

"It is hurtful. Don't say it again."

The broken record technique usually ends with the other person giving up. In fact, if you think about it this is often a technique used by PA people themselves to get you to give up on your confrontation.

Method 5. Direct confrontation

Sometimes you might decide that the best way of handling PA behavior is to directly confront. This is especially true when you know that the behavior is intentionally hurtful. However, any confrontation still needs to follow the rules especially remaining calm, being assertive, and choosing your words carefully. For instance, "I feel insulted (hurt). Is that your intention?" can be effective for a variety of PA comments that are hurtful or insulting.

Keep in mind that most PA people are good at evading or misdirecting a direct confrontation, so you need to be prepared to make your point no matter how they respond. If you let them control the situation, you are likely to fall into their trap of escalating the situation and you looking like the instigator because you caused the conflict by confronting.

Method 6. Consequences to behavior

Another way of responding to PA behavior is through consequences. For instance, if you determine that the person is not receptive or if they are malicious, walk away. Don't give them the reward of being drawn into their PA game.

Sometimes it may not be possible to completely walk away, in which case you need to set limits. Do not be shy to set these limits clearly and loudly "Stop!" or "I'm not going to discuss this." Many PA people, especially the malicious ones, count on you to be "too" nice. Instead, being firm can sometimes stop their behavior.

Another way to set limits when someone's PA behavior interferes with something you are doing is to stop doing it. For example, you ask for help doing the laundry and your family member responds in a PA manner--don't do their laundry. Or, when someone is trying to get attention through PA behavior-- don't give them attention.

Method 7. Reward desired behavior

When you start ignoring or confronting the PA behavior, it becomes easier to reward desired behavior. The more you reward the behavior you want to see, the more likely it will continue, and hopefully, replace the PA behavior. If the PA person learns that direct communication is more likely to get results, then they may become more direct. For instance, if the person makes a direct rather than PA statement, reward it by responding to it quickly and positively. "I'm so glad you reminded me! I'll get right to it." Or, when they do something to be helpful without the attached negativity, thank them! Notice appropriate behavior and try to be responsive to it when you can.

Method 8. Be passive-aggressive

When all else fails, be passive-aggressive yourself. However, you should only use this method in the case where you don't care about the ongoing relationship such as dealing with a PA malicious person.

This technique can be tricky so you need to be very skilled and know exactly what you are doing. You don't want to be drawn into a PA one-up-manship game. Instead, you want a response that will shut them down. This means that you need to put them into a PA trap from which they can't escape without calling attention to their behavior or looking like the bad guy. In other words, their choice is to either become more directly aggressive or to give up. When they get more aggressive, they look like the bad guy and appear to be responsible for the problem which is contrary to what they are trying to achieve.

I've sometimes used this method when I receive mean and unhelpful comments on my Android apps. Such comments are PA because even though the comments could be considered aggressive, the method of anonymity (and therefore, not being responsible) makes it PA. Sometimes people are sincerely reviewing the apps and their word choice may be unpleasant, in which case, I appreciate the message and ignore the tone. Other times they are just mean. Using a response such as "Kindly explain to me what you mean and I will take it into consideration" addresses both situations. If the person is sincere and truly wants to be helpful, this statement is likely to open a dialog. However, for those who are being PA, this statement is a PA response in return which provides no reward for them, and if they continue, makes them look like a bully. Therefore, my response forces them to either get more aggressive or to give up. By the way, they almost never respond if their intention is malicious.

Using these rules and methods won't solve all your problems with PA people, but you are more likely to feel in control and less doubtful of yourself when dealing with PA people.

Chapter 3

Why Are People Mean? Don't Take It Personally!

"Why are people so mean?" seems to be a plaintive cry across the internet. Although the issue may be more prevalent online due to the anonymity and accessibility, it is by no means limited to the online community. Yet, other people's "meanness" impacts us more than it really needs to. The more that people can recognize that the meanness they experience from others is either unintentional or is more about the mean person rather than about them, the less they personalize the meanness and the less impact it has on them.

What is Personalizing?

Fran focused on doing a good job at work and because she tended to not spend much time chatting with her co-workers she tended to accomplish a great deal. In fact, it was apparent to everyone that she was able to complete more tasks than her co-workers who spent a great deal of time on their phones, playing on the internet, and talking with one another. One day, one of her co-workers came out of the supervisor's office and verbally attacked Fran: "I just got in trouble and it's all your fault! You make everyone else look bad by being such a brown-noser." Fran, shocked and hurt, felt bad about herself because someone was angry with her.

Obviously, Fran hadn't done anything wrong. The problem in this situation was the co-worker who was directing her anger at Fran rather than taking responsibility for her own behavior. This misdirected self-protective behavior often occurs when someone has problems with insecurity which frequently leads to jealousy and blame.

However, even though Fran wasn't wrong, she still suffered the consequences of the co-worker's wrath. In fact, this is the purpose of such behavior, by blaming the problem on someone else and causing them to feel bad, the co-worker could feel better.

Personalization is interpreting someone's behavior as being about you or due to you and then feeling bad about yourself. If Fran could recognize that the co-worker's attack was due to the co-worker's personal problems and had nothing to do with her, she could more easily shrug it off and not suffer the consequences of it.

Why Are So Many People Mean?

I don't believe most people are mean people. However, under the right circumstances, most people can be mean. For example, about 50 years ago Milgram conducted his famous "obedience" studies which involved telling the subject that a person in the next room was attached to a machine that delivered electric shock (unknown to the subject, the device was not actually attached). The subject was to ask this person questions and to deliver a shock by flipping a switch on the machine in front of them. The device had a dial on it clearly labeled from mild to dangerous. The researcher told the subject to increase the amount of shock with each wrong answer.

Although most people deny that they would turn the dial to dangerous and shock someone when told to do so, Milgram found that nearly 70% of the subjects obeyed the researcher and increased the shock to the dangerous range even when they heard screaming, and finally silence, from the next room. This type of study is not allowed to be conducted today due to the potential psychological harm to the subject from knowing they could cause harm to another human being.

Most of you reading this are probably trying to rationalize right now why you would not be among that 70% or you are thinking that something must have been different about those people who were subjects in the study. However, the research and other similar research was conducted with different variations showing the same type of outcome.

I believe that this research shows what I stated earlier, that under the right circumstances most people can be mean. The circumstance in this research was the pressure to obey, the pressure to conform, the stress of the situation, and the fear of authority. These are only some of the circumstances that may contribute to people doing "mean" things even when they are not "mean" people.

Mean People Are Noticeable

Often there appears to be so many mean people in the world around us, because the behavior of mean people tends to be more noticeable. One reason for this is probably the way our brains are wired for survival. According to Rick Hanson, author of Buddha's Brain, we need to be especially observant of the negative things in our environment because those are the things that are most likely to harm us. As a result, those most likely to survive and pass their genes to the next generation were those who were particularly sensitive to danger in the environment.

Another reason mean people are more noticeable is that their behavior is often particularly offensive and hurtful. We are more likely to notice and dwell on the person who cut us off in traffic rather than the person who let us merge. The more malicious the behavior, the more likely we are to be distressed and to dwell on what occurred.

However, this supports my position that meanness isn't the norm. For instance, notice what stories make the news. The nature of news is that it is unusual or it has an extreme impact on people's lives. A good example is that the West Nile virus that had significantly fewer episodes and fatalities than the flu got much more media attention. Or a major airplane crash, because it is so rare, will get extensive coverage. And certainly, anything negative tends to generate more media focus than positive things. Therefore, since meanness gets our attention, I would propose that it is actually rarer than niceness but more noticeable.

Meanness is Rewarded

Unfortunately, another aspect of meanness that makes it more visible is that it is often rewarded. Sometimes the reward can be tangible such as a ruthless businessman being rewarded by making more money. However, it can also be rewarded with attention or escalation of conflict. It varies with each person what sort of reward is meaningful, although for meanness to continue there must be some sort of reward to the perpetrator. We will examine this further as we look at the different reasons for meanness.

Unintentional vs. Malicious Meanness

Although I tried to organize the types of reasons for being "mean" from unintentional to malicious, I recognize that a case can be made for maliciousness or unintentional meanness in almost any of the categories. However, I believe that, in general, the following categories represent a continuum of meanness from unintentional to malicious.

Unintentional meanness refers to behavior or statements that the recipient may perceive as mean but that weren't intended to be hurtful. Whereas malicious meanness is behavior or statements that have the purpose of hurting the recipient. The idea of a continuum is that most mean behavior is a mixture of intentionality. Also, much of intentional meanness may not be severe enough in its impact to be considered malicious. Therefore, malicious meanness for the purpose of this article and the categories I have created is considered both intended and extreme.

Reasons for Meanness

The following reasons for meanness are listed in order, to the best of my ability, from the unintentional situations that may be perceived as being mean, to the reactive situations in which people are mean, to the situations with malicious intentions.

Reason 1: Lack of Skills/Knowledge or Awareness

Frequently people will perceive a behavior as mean when there was no intention to be hurtful. Instead, the behavior may be due to a lack of skills, a lack of knowledge, or a lack of awareness. It is important to be able to determine if this may be the case because there are many situations in which people appear mean for these reasons when they have no such intention. By understanding when this occurs you are able to eliminate these situations from your perception of the amount of "meanness" in the world around you and are less likely to be insulted.

Lack of Awareness

Not Noticing

Sometimes others may be focused internally or on something else and don't notice your situation. For example, someone doesn't let you merge in traffic because their attention is focused on their companion and they don't notice that you want to merge. Certainly, you could make a case that they should be paying more attention in traffic. However, the evidence isn't available that they were being mean; instead they were unaware.

Cultural

Also, lack of awareness is often involved with cultural differences. For instance, a great deal of misunderstandings occur because of personal space. Research has shown that in the U.S. people stand about three to twelve feet away from one another unless they are romantically involved. Someone from another culture who stands much closer may be interpreted as intimidating or rude. By recognizing that people have different belief systems and behavior when interacting with others, we can understand that their behavior may not be "mean," but has a different meaning in their culture.

Little Insight

Some people may have little insight or awareness of how they impact others. They might tend to be more concrete in their thought processes and don't realize their behavior may be hurtful or rude. For example, a simple question such as "How old are you?" may have much undercurrent of meaning. Some people are insulted by the question because they believe it implies they are old. Someone with little insight about others' feelings may not realize that they insulted someone.

Lack of Skills

Social Skills

Some people may have poor social skills. They may not have been taught the proper social skills or they may not have the experience with social interaction to have learned the skills. As a result, they may be awkward interacting with others. For instance, someone who is shy or who has Asperger's Syndrome may not make adequate eye contact. Some people may interpret this as lack of interest and be insulted.

Some people may not know certain skills such as solving problems assertively. When they are attempting to learn these skills they may not be able to find the right words or tone of voice that comes with more experience. When people are first learning these skills they may appear more aggressive than they intend.

Tone

Some people have difficulty in communication because they lack the skill of expressing the right tone. This can occur in spoken communication but especially is problematic with written communication. These days of the internet, email, and texting have led to numerous problems due to the fact that tone cannot be easily conveyed through these mediums. I have had clients read emails or texts to me they maintained were insulting; and certainly, when read with the tone of voice they used, they were insulting. However, when I read the emails out loud without the tone, the message was entirely different.

Another problem is that certain types of humor or sarcasm can be very difficult to use the right tone and can be easily misunderstood. For instance, I have a very dry sense of humor that can work well with the proper non-verbals but is difficult to communicate in writing. I made the mistake when I first wrote articles for my website to write the way I communicate verbally. I made a joke that a reader mistook as an attempt to manipulate and was highly insulted. Therefore, when I write now I try to keep in mind that people from different backgrounds all over the world will be reading my articles. I can't prevent all misunderstandings but I can stay away from teasing and dry humor which can be easily misunderstood.

Reason 2: Miscommunication/Misunderst anding

Communication involves at least two people. At any particular point, one person is conveying information and the other is receiving information. Problems can occur anywhere in the process. Miscommunication is when the individual conveying information makes errors in the process of communicating. Such errors can include inaccurate word choice, non-verbals that aren't in sync with the words used, not taking into consideration the audience and possible interpretations based on the characteristics of the listener. Misunderstanding is when the receiver of the information misinterprets the communication.

Communication problems are usually not intentional and by resolving the inaccuracy in the communication, the problem can usually be resolved. I worked with a husband and wife once who were aggressively arguing for a good part of the session. I noticed that both of them kept using the same word in their argument and I asked them each to define it for me. What they discovered is that they had totally different definitions of the word and by understanding the other's definition they were able to resolve the argument.

Negative Assumptions

A common reason for misinterpretation are assumptions made by the listener. Sometimes these assumptions are as simple as believing they know what is going to be said and respond without listening thoroughly. Other times they may negatively interpret based upon their own biases or fears.

For instance, someone with social anxiety may interpret "I'm busy tomorrow and can't have lunch with you" as meaning "I don't like you."

When someone engages in this type of assumption making, often referred to as "mind-reading" because they think they know what the other person is really thinking, they may sometimes react accordingly. For instance, the person who believes that the other person doesn't like him/her may tend to withdraw. Reactions due to these assumptions may lead to more negative consequences such as the other person perceiving him or her as unfriendly.

Directness/Indirectness

Directness

Some people have a very direct approach in their communication because they recognize that hinting or indirect communication often leads to misunderstandings. However, this direct approach can be interpreted by the recipient as being mean. For instance, directly stating "I'm not interested in dating you. Thank you anyway" can be viewed as mean when in reality it may be less hurtful than the indirect approach of not returning phone calls.

Indirectness

The indirect approach is often used because the communicator does not want to hurt the other person's feelings or wants to avoid conflict. However, this approach often leads to a great deal of miscommunication and often more hurt feelings in the long run.

Lack of Social Anxiety

Some people who lack social anxiety may be fairly blunt in their communications because such directness would not affect them negatively. Therefore, it doesn't occur to them that such communication may be offensive to some people. In fact, most of us communicate with others in a way that would be okay with us and don't consider that other people may respond better to a different approach. So, we treat others the way we would like to be treated rather than treating them the way they would like to be treated. And when we are really clueless we tell them the problem is that they are "too sensitive."

Reason 3: Misdirected Intentions

Helpfulness

Frequently we may perceive someone as being hurtful when they are actually trying to be helpful. This can occur, for example, when a parent is being over-protective or when a boss is reviewing someone's work excessively. It is easy to misinterpret these attempts to help as offensive or insulting. However, in these cases the individual is not intentionally hurtful and frequently the situation can be resolved by discussing the problem.

My husband is a person who wants to help others by giving advice and warning them about pitfalls in what they are attempting to do. Sometimes this can be quite annoying because it feels as if he is saying "I don't think you are capable" or "I don't trust you to consider this thoroughly" when he is actually intending to be helpful and to protect others from making mistakes and suffering the consequences. This used to cause a great deal of conflict for us until I realized that he has the good intentions of helping me and protecting me. In fact, he used to say "Listen to my intentions. Not my words." Once I learned to do that much conflict was resolved.

More intentional, but not meant to hurt, is when someone believes they need to "toughen" someone up by being firm or even aggressive. This type of reasoning we need to be cautious about interpreting too innocuously because sometimes it is used as an excuse to be mean.

Necessary of Outcome

Sometimes people may believe that they have to act a certain way in order to achieve the outcome they want. For example, a boss may believe that he/she may have to be harsh and threatening for people to do their work. An old movie that shows this in action is "An Officer and a Gentleman" in which the Sargent believed that he had to break the recruit down so as to reshape him and help him.

In these situations, the intention may be good, but the process may be unnecessary as there may be other, less harsh ways, of obtaining the same outcome.

Principled

Some people have certain beliefs that have good intentions but may appear to be mean to others. One such belief is the desire to be completely honest and genuine in all interactions with others. This may sound nice on the surface but in actual practice it may appear to be mean. For example, "I think that dress makes you look fat" may be honest but it is likely to cause hurt feelings.

Many people who have this type of thinking don't realize they are making a choice in their manner of being honest. They think that being genuine is stating whatever thought occurs to them because otherwise they are pretending and false. However, this is not necessarily true because we have all sorts of thoughts that we may discard because they are not accurate. In addition, it is possible to be truthful without hurting other people's feelings. For instance, "I think this other dress is so much more attractive on you" can be honest as well but not hurtful.

Reason 4: Self-Protection

The last several reasons for meanness that I described have primarily been unintentional and that often just understanding this can lead to less perception of meanness and less reactivity. However, self-protection and the next several reasons for meanness have some degree of intentionality although sometimes it may be subconscious. Even though some people in this category can be malicious in their meanness, most of the time they are desperately trying to protect themselves and survive albeit in a not very effective way.

Meanness in the case of self-protection is due to the individual's inability to take responsibility for their problems and to do something about it. With self-protection we see a wide range of severity of meanness. The healthier people try to recognize when they are mean, apologize and make amends, and try to make changes. However, no one is perfect so they may continue to make mistakes. But at least they recognize the mistakes. Whereas the less healthy people are completely ignorant of their responsibility for their behavior and don't try to make improvements.

The following is a list of reasons that people engage in self-protective meanness. Now please understand I'm not saying any of these reasons are right but by understanding the reasons we can reduce the impact on us as well as handle them more effectively. When dealing with these types of people, it is important to recognize that they are being mean because of their personal flaws, not because anything is wrong with you. For some of these people, the problem may be resolved by confronting the behavior.

Low Self-esteem

Many, but not all, people with low self-esteem may act to protect their fragile self-esteem especially those who are unaware of their low self-esteem. They may be hurting emotionally, and unfortunately, an effective way to feel better is to feel superior to someone else. So there are a number of ways that this may occur.

Projection

Instead of admitting shortcomings, people may project them onto other people and accuse them of the behavior they don't acknowledge in themselves. For instance, someone who is dishonest may perceive everyone else as liars and thieves and accuse them of trying to take advantage of him or her.

Superiority Complex

Some people who are unable to acknowledge their low self-esteem may compensate by acting as if they are better than others. Their meanness may often be sarcastic or even direct put-downs such as "It's so obvious. Anyone with an ounce of brains would know that."

Passive-aggressive Escalation

A method used for self-protection is passive-aggressive escalation. The purpose of this behavior is to aggress in such an indirect way that it causes the recipient to react and look like the bad guy. My article "Crazy-Makers: Dealing With Passive-Aggressive People" describes this process in more detail.

Jealousy

Some people with low self-esteem may engage in meanness out of jealousy. They tend to be insecure and might try to criticize others in an attempt to feel better about themselves. For instance, "She thinks she's so much better than us—look at how she flaunts herself with those expensive clothes."

Rationalization

Attempts to defend the self-esteem by supplying logical reasons rather than acknowledging and taking responsibility for the real reason are known as rationalizations. For example, someone is fired and states "I didn't kiss up to the boss" rather than recognizing that poor performance was the cause.

Intellectualization of Emotions

Many people are uncomfortable with intense emotions and try to reduce the intensity in various ways. One way of doing this is intellectualization which is focusing on the less emotional internal processes rather than feeling the emotions. For example, someone focuses on the details of arranging a funeral rather than the feelings of grief due to their loss.

Sometimes this intellectualization can be perceived as mean because it may lack empathy or connection with another person's feelings. Other people may take this as meaning that the person doesn't care or even that their feelings are being ridiculed. For instance, someone not comfortable with emotions might comment "Why are you so upset?"

Controlling

Some people protect themselves by trying to control others. They are trying to create a comfortable world for themselves. In the process they may cause a great deal of discomfort for others.

Anxiety

When people are anxious and fearful they may tend to avoid situations that cause anxiety. Sometimes they might try to control those close to them so as to avoid anxiety. For example, a husband who is afraid of being perceived as weak may be critical of his wife in front of others.

Or, a woman who is afraid of having anxiety or panic if she's alone may control her family's activities by wanting them to stay with her.

What makes this type of situation more "mean" is when the anxiety is not acknowledged and the method of control is indirect such as using guilt: "You don't really care about me. You don't want to be around me."

Need to Be Right

Some people try to protect their self image by being perfect. They might believe that living the perfect life proves their worth. Unfortunately, some may also have the need to point out to others their "perfectness" by disparaging others. This need to be right is controlling because it has the effect of silencing others when they might disagree. Therefore, the meanness is self-protective because it prevents opposing opinions from intruding into their view of themselves in the world.

Validation

You have probably heard the saying "Misery loves company." For some people who are miserable, validating or confirming their negative view of the world helps them to feel less miserable because they can feel good about their assessment: "See, people are only out to take advantage of others." They prove their view by being mean which is likely to generate meanness in return.

Trust Issues

Many people who have been seriously hurt or traumatized may feel that others cannot be trusted and have developed methods of self-protection in order to survive. Some of those methods may be perceived as mean whereas other methods may actually be hurtful.

Withdrawal

A common way to deal with lack of trust in others is to withdraw from contact with others. Withdrawal can be complete social isolation, but since that is very difficult to achieve in a world where we must rely on others withdrawal is often more subtle. It may be avoidance of certain types of situations or interactions with others.

Sometimes this withdrawal may be perceived as mean by others because they don't understand the underlying fear causing the behavior. All they see is how the person acts. For instance, Ann who had been abused as a child and was in an abusive marriage turned down invitations to lunch by co-workers. She was afraid that her husband would become jealous of a friendship and fly into a violent rage. However, her co-workers didn't know the reason; they just thought she was unfriendly.

Identifying With the Abuser

Occasionally when someone has been abused they survive by identifying with the abuser and modeling their behavior. The purpose of this is that they see the abuser as powerful and they want to be in control so that no one can hurt them again. They don't trust other people based on their experience with abuse and believe that the only way they can protect themselves is to be powerful. However, this type of person can cause considerable harm to others because they have become an abuser, too.

Vulnerability

Another way abused people protect themselves is to avoid being vulnerable. They may do this by showing a "tough" front which may come across as rude or mean. Sometimes they believe that politeness demonstrates weakness and don't want to appear "weak" to others.

Reason 5: Reactive

One of the most common reasons for meanness is due to emotional reaction. In such situations the person may just be reacting without thinking through the impact of their reaction. Therefore, often their focus may not be for the purpose of hurting someone else although it can be. Also, the reaction can sometimes be quite severe and harmful. Therefore, it is included more towards the malicious end of the continuum.

Frustration

When someone is frustrated with a situation they may react in a manner to release tension. When this reaction is directed against someone else, it can be considered mean. For instance, a wife hits her shin against a piece of equipment in the garage and then yells at her husband and blames him for stuffing the garage full of equipment.

Stress related

Unmanaged stress increases the physical symptoms of tension including muscular tension and a heightened state of agitation. Attempts to reduce this discomfort may result in mean behavior.

Displacement

Sometimes people inappropriately transfer their aggression to someone who did not cause their stress in an attempt to alleviate the discomfort. A classic example is a man who is reprimanded by his boss. He doesn't want to risk his job by defending himself. However, when he comes home he yells at his wife for some insignificant thing, who in turn yells at the kid, who then kicks the dog. They have all displaced their anger onto someone who is not the source of the anger but is a safer target.

Denial

Another way of attempting to reduce stress is through denial. However, the process of denial can potentially be mean to someone else. For example, a wife doesn't want to deal with her overspending problem and ignores the fact that they are going more into debt. Eventually their house is foreclosed on because she had not told her husband she hadn't been paying the bills.

Reason 6: Superiority

Feelings of superiority can lead to mean behavior that may not always be deliberate but can be very hurtful to others.

Superior by Birth

Different from a superiority complex that stems from low self-esteem, some people truly believe they are superior to others. Sometimes this is due to being taught from a young age that being born into privilege or money or with certain qualities makes them better than other people. Some who believe this feel that they have an obligation to treat those lesser than them with respect. However, others may have disdain for those they perceive as less than them and treat them with a lack of understanding or compassion.

Superior by Achievement

Some people who have achieved success early in life and easily may also develop this attitude of superiority. Due to their success they are often treated as if they are better than others and they may come to believe that they deserve to be treated this way by everyone. Therefore, they may be rude and demanding.

Moral Superiority

Finally, some people have a sense of superiority because of their beliefs. For instance, they may have a sense of moral superiority such as people discussed earlier who believe that total honesty, no matter how hurtful, is being genuine. Or, people who believe that they are always right so their opinion is more valid than others' opinions. Or, someone who rebels against the status quo or against being politically correct because they believe it is phoney. These people believe in their right to behave in ways that might hurt other people because they are doing it for morally superior reasons.

Reason 7: Mental Disturbance

Being mean due to mental problems is nearer to the malicious end of the continuum because of the severity of the events that can occur. However, it is very important to recognize that most people who have mental illness are not mean or are probably more in the self-protective category if they are mean. This category is referring to those people who have severe mental disturbance causing them to be mean.

Mental Illness

Although someone who has mental illness may be unintentional in their meanness, they can sometimes be quite hurtful. For example, a person with paranoid schizophrenia may become very anxious in certain situations and react with a great deal of anger against undeserving targets. Sometimes this can reach the level of physical aggression. I do need to reiterate, however, that most people with mental illness and even paranoid schizophrenia are not hurtful to others.

Other times people with mental illness can be mean indirectly. For instance, a woman with obsessive-compulsive disorder who demands that her family engage in excessive cleaning behavior such as showering before they come into the house. If they don't comply, she becomes very angry in her attempt to control them.

Psychopathy

The worst of the meanness due to mental disturbance is psychopathy. A psychopath is usually quite intentional in their meanness and often malicious. This type of person may also derive pleasure from meanness and would therefore be in the next category as well.

A psychopath is often the most dangerous type of person because they can frequently be very charming and disarming. Often you may not know you are dealing with a psychopath until it is too late. Fortunately, the type of psychopath that you see in movies who is physically dangerous is more rare. However, psychopath refers to anyone who doesn't have a conscience and is willing to take advantage of other people for their own personal gain without feeling any regret. Therefore, they can cause a great deal of harm whether they are a salesperson or a politician or a criminal.

Reason 8: Pleasure-seeking

I placed the pleasure-seeking reason as the most intentional and malicious of the reasons for being mean because I find it most disturbing. Even though some of the behaviors may not be excessive, people who act mean based on this reason are doing so due to a self-centeredness and complete disregard of others. They seek to feel good at the expense of others. The following categories are based upon the type of reward they obtain by being mean.

Attention

Frequently people engage in mean behavior because of the attention they gain. Attention doesn't even have to be positive to be rewarding. We see this frequently in children who misbehave and are mean to others because they get noticed. Unfortunately, some people never grow up and continue to hurt others in adulthood for the purpose of obtaining notice.

Respect

Some people confuse respect with fear. They believe that if they mistreat someone they will gain respect. However, what they achieve is obedience based on fear. For example, a boss who threatens employees with termination for minor problems to keep them in line. Or, a parent who states "My children respect my authority because I'm willing to use the belt."

Power

One of the most rewarding aspects of being mean is obtaining power. Making someone else hurt or react gives them control over that person and allows them to feel more powerful. The attempt to gain power can be either direct and aggressive or it can be passive-aggressive. Sometimes the passive-aggressive is more difficult to recognize.

For example, someone makes a casual statement such as: "I'm surprised you handled that situation so well." If the recipient reacts negatively to the hidden insult, the passive-aggressive person might state: "I don't understand why you are acting like this. All I did was give you a compliment." At that point they have gained control over the recipient's emotional reaction which gives them power.

Money

Some circumstances reward meanness with monetary gain. For instance, someone who profits from insider trading to the detriment of the shareholders of a company. Or, people who trash their competitor's products online to improve their own sales.

Conclusion

As you see from the above reasons, most people are mean due to some flaw in themselves or distortion in their thinking. Usually, unless you have done something significant, it is not about you. Notice that I say "something significant." People who are mean will often find some minor thing that you have done so as to justify their meanness and blame you.

Therefore, if even one of these reasons can apply to a situation, you need to recognize that you are not at fault for the way someone treats you. By recognizing that you don't deserve to be treated that way, you may prevent yourself from feeling as bad. Certainly, it hurts when someone is particularly malicious in their behavior, but understanding that it is due to a disturbance in them and not about you can help you cope.

However, just because you don't deserve to be treated meanly, don't respond with mean behavior. That only validates and rewards the person who is mean by giving them permission to behave meanly in return. Attention and escalation of the conflict rewards the mean behavior because it allows them to place the blame on you.

The main purpose of this article is to help people recognize that meanness is rewarded when the attack is successful. But it needs the recipient's participation to be successful. In other words, when the recipient feels bad about him or herself, the meanness has been successful.

Therefore, what you can do is to not participate. Recognize that unless you have done something that clearly hurts someone else, you are not the cause of the meanness. Don't base your self-worth on someone else's opinion or treatment of you. Don't feel bad about yourself when someone is mean to you. Instead, pity them or feel sad for them that their experience of the world is so negative and limited. They are likely to experience the consequences of their meanness and won't live very happy lives. Remember "Living well is the best revenge (George Herbert)." Focus on living your life and don't get involved in the pettiness of mean people.

Chapter 4

How You Can Be More Resistant to Workplace Bullying

Bullying at work can often be so subtle that it is difficult to report without appearing to be overly sensitive or petty. Most people are not overtly bullied with physical attacks or threats of violence because these behaviors can be easily identified and reported. Instead, most bullying at work is a passive-aggressive type that is usually a combination of subtle behaviors that the perpetrator can easily deny as being misunderstood.

Some examples

Withholding. A co-worker doesn't provide you with necessary information for a task and your performance is affected. The co-worker can claim they didn't realize you didn't have the information.

Excessive oversight. Your boss monitors your work constantly, questioning everything that you do. Your boss can claim that is his/her management style or that s/he was concerned about the project and your performance.

Gossip. It is especially difficult to control or report gossip because it can be unclear who started it and it is whispered behind your back.

Facial expressions. How do you report sarcastic facial expressions? "She rolls her eyes whenever I voice an opinion" may be difficult to prove without appearing sensitive.

Teasing. The same behavior can have two different meanings when a person is teased by a friend or by someone they don't get along with. The bully can claim that it was just friendly teasing and it wasn't meant to hurt.

Frequent criticism. Your boss focuses on your mistakes, is quick to point out errors but doesn't give you credit for successes.

As you can see from some of the examples, it may be difficult to eliminate workplace bullying because it just becomes more passive-aggressive and hidden. Also, it may not be any one behavior but a combination of events that add up to bullying. A person knows they are being bullied by how the behavior makes them feel but it can be difficult to pinpoint the exact behaviors when the bullying is passive-aggressive.

Yet, workplace bullying can have profound effects on the recipients including anxiety and/or depression or even post-traumatic stress disorder. It can undermine a person's confidence, affect their performance, and preclude them from consideration for promotions.

However, some people are more resistant to workplace bullying so that it doesn't have the impact upon them. Learning to be resistant can prevent bullies from being rewarded for their behavior by hindering their agenda which may even change their behavior when their attempts to bully backfires.

Research shows that certain personality styles are more resistant to bullying (Plopa et al., 2017). Although personality styles tend to be stable over time due to the genetics of being born with certain temperaments, the specific behaviors natural to certain personalities can be learned and used by those with other styles. Therefore, no matter your personality style you can still develop a resistance to bullying.

Personality configurations and vulnerability to bullying

The cooperative achiever

This style is resistant to bullying and depicts those who tend to have a stable mood with low anxiety, high agreeableness, and high conscientiousness. People who are highly agreeable tend to give others the benefit of the doubt. Instead of interpreting behavior as negative and hurtful, they are more likely to interpret it as unintentional or that the person is under stress or having a bad day. In this way, they do not take the behavior personally and are less likely to be reactive to it. When high conscientiousness is combined with emotional stability and agreeableness, the person is motivated and persistent with a positive attitude toward work. They are likely to be cooperative with others and to seek help or social support when needed. They usually trust others, are compassionate and concerned about others, thus having good interpersonal relationships.

The social optimist

This style is also resistant to bullying and describes someone who is emotionally stable, outgoing and is open to new experiences. This person tends to be self-confident, social, composed, resistant to stress, more likely to seek social support if needed and less likely to interpret events in a negative way. When this style is combined with high conscientiousness it depicts the entrepreneurial type of personality with a high degree of psychological flexibility which is least vulnerable to stress and bullying.

The disagreeable perfectionist

This style with its emotional instability, low agreeableness, and high conscientiousness is vulnerable to workplace bullying. Often considered a "double-edged sword", conscientiousness can be protective when focusing on work is used to distract from and alleviate the stress of the emotional environment. However, when conscientiousness is combined with perfectionistic expectations, negativity, and disagreeableness, well-being suffers in the face of bullying. People with this style tend to be obstinate, determined, prone to verbal aggression but less likely to engage in physical aggression due to the conscientiousness holding them to a higher standard. A person who is highly conscientious but also negative often suffers from low self-esteem or will focus the negativity outward by blaming others for not doing things right. As a result of their disagreeableness and demands of others they are also more likely to create a negative reaction from others.

The socially anxious nonconformist

This individual may be anxious and shy but also tends to be unconventional and open to new experience. This combination makes them more vulnerable to bullying. People who are open to experience tend to feel both negative and positive emotions intensely. When combined with optimism, emotional stability, and extraversion this quality tends to be protective because they are able to experience more positive emotions and are able to release negative emotions through social support. However, when combined with social anxiety and withdrawal, their unconventional attitudes may cause them to stand out in a more negative way and be susceptible to bullying. Thus, this individual experiences stress due to feeling pulled in different directions: a desire to be different but anxiety about being noticed in a negative manner.

What are the behaviors of the resistant personalities that can be learned?

You may not be able to change your personality, but by copying the behaviors of these personality styles you may be able to reduce the impact of workplace bullying. Personality may be set to some degree by genetics but behavior is a choice and can be learned.

For instance, I had a client who was socially anxious, introverted, and depressed, all characteristics that made her more vulnerable to bullying, who was being bullied and sexually harassed by her boss. Reporting his behaviors was not effective because the behaviors were subtle and subject to interpretation. So we focused on her being direct and assertive with him. When he engaged in any inappropriate behaviors, she identified those behaviors to him and told him they were inappropriate. If he protested that he didn't mean anything by his behavior, she told him, "Whether or not you intend to hurt me, I'm telling you that it does and I want you to stop." Although initially she was convinced she would lose her job, not only did he stop harassing her but he promoted her to a leadership position.

There are a number of behaviors the resistant personalities may engage in naturally. However, these protective behaviors can also be learned by other personalities:

Seek social support. A primary way of coping with stress is through the support of others—having someone to talk to or get advice from or commiserate with improves resistance to bullying. An introvert does not need a large social group but they can benefit from a few or even one trusted associate.

Pleasant. Being pleasant with a positive focus on others can help a person resist bullying. One reason for this is that the agenda of a bully is to create conflict or distress so when they are unable to do this their behavior may backfire by causing them to feel frustrated. In addition, being generally pleasant will cause others to be more supportive of you and less likely to validate the bully.

Optimistic. An optimist tends to expect positive outcomes so in the face of bullying they tend to look for ways to problem-solve. Instead of focusing on the negative aspects of the situation they tend to find ways to manage it effectively.

Positive interpretations. Those who are resistant to bullying tend to make positive or at least neutral interpretations of the bully's behavior. One type of interpretation is that they are less likely to see themselves as the cause of others' negative behavior. They also may be more likely to view the bully in a more compassionate way instead of seeing the behavior as malicious. One way of doing this is to recognize that many of us have reacted in hurtful ways when stressed.

Non-perfectionistic effort. Those who resist bullying are unlikely to be perfectionists. Instead, they strive for excellence but can accept mistakes. Instead of failure contributing to a negative self-concept they see it as an opportunity to learn and change. They are persistent in their efforts because they don't accept failure as a reason to quit. For more, read: Excellence vs. Perfection.

Psychologically flexible. Having the ability to adapt and change behavior when a situation calls for it helps a person to be more resistant to bullying. Instead of focusing on expecting others or the situation to change they focus on what they have control of which typically is their own behavior. As a result, they are more likely to find solutions. For more, read: Coping with Change: Psychological Flexibility.

Positive self-concept. Those who are resistant to bullying are likely to have a positive self-concept so the bullying is less likely to affect their self-confidence or perspective of themselves. Instead, they see the bullying as a problem in the other person and find ways to protect themselves from it. For more on changing the self-concept, read: 20 Steps to Better Self-Esteem.

What can be done when you are bullied at work?

In addition to making yourself less vulnerable to bullying by developing more of the above behaviors, the following list some steps you can take to manage the situation.

Promote yourself. Write down your accomplishments and how you are an asset to the business. When you write your achievements it reminds you of the truth about yourself and your work performance. As a result you are more likely to promote yourself and your accomplishments to those in positions that matter. Don't allow bullying to let you become passive or decrease your confidence. Build yourself up so that you can see the reality.

Be assertive. Learn communication skills to effectively manage passive-aggressive behavior. Confront behavior but do it in a way that works. For more, read the Chapter: 7 Rules and 8 Methods for Responding to Passive-aggressive People.

Document patterns. Usually bullying isn't just one instance but a pattern of behavior. So document the behaviors that occur and be sure to include your responses showing how you tried to handle it. When documenting write a word for word account and specific behavior descriptions without your interpretation. For instance, instead of writing "He tried to humiliate me," write "He pointed out my mistake repeatedly in a group setting saying 'I can't believe you did this.'"

Report. Once you have the documentation and your efforts have not changed the situation, get assistance by reporting the behavior.

Reference

Plopa, M., Plopa, W. and Skuzinska, A. (2017). Bullying at Work, Personality and Subjective Well-Being. Journal of Occupational Health Psychology, 22, 19–27. DOI:10.1037/a0040320

Chapter 5

Are You Passive-Aggressive and Want to Change?

Most of us are passive-aggressive (PA) at times. Although much of the communication literature tells us we should be direct and assertive, I've always told my clients there is a time and place for different communication styles. For instance, if you've had your car in to a repair shop several times for the same problem and they want to charge you for fixing it again, being verbally aggressive might accomplish your agenda. Or, if you are confronted by an irrational angry person, a self-protective passive response of walking away may be best.

I've always taught that the communication style you choose should be based on the outcome you want. For instance, with the mechanic you might not care about your long-term relationship—you just want your car fixed, so an aggressive stance may work. But aggression is not a good choice in a relationship you care about.

The same is true of PA communication. It is generally not a good choice for relationships that are important to you. Notice that I'm referring to "choice." Most people act without thinking. They have long-standing behavior patterns and may not even be aware of their own PA behavior. But it is a choice to continue to engage in these patterns of behavior.

Although most people readily acknowledge they don't like being on the receiving end of PA behavior because it is so frustrating and unpleasant, many people are slow to label their own PA behavior. Instead they often justify their actions by focusing completely on the other person's behavior. Yet, sometimes when people read about others' PA behavior, they begin to recognize their own behavior.

If communication problems are interfering with your relationships, it might be a good idea to examine whether you have PA behavior. By recognizing when you are PA you can change your pattern and develop better relationships. The following can help you more thoroughly examine your behavior and create a plan to change. Many PA behaviors are unintentional but they are still hurtful to the relationship. Other PA behaviors may be deliberately calculated to hurt the other person.

Those who are PA and want to change are usually unintentionally PA. In other words, they are not trying to maliciously cause problems for others and/or don't care about how they hurt others. Sometimes they may even have good intentions such as not wanting to hurt someone's feelings or cause a problem. But instead of direct communication about problems they engage in PA behavior. So the following focuses mainly on the unintentional type of passive-aggressiveness. What is the Purpose of Unintentional Passive-Aggressive Behavior?

Usually unintentional PA behavior is either self-protective in some way or it is learned behavior. Such PA behavior can occur for a number of reasons:

Learned communication patterns. Unless we deliberately seek out new methods of communication, we tend to use the ones that we learned when we were children. So if someone grows up in a family where PA behavior is the primary communication method they are likely to use the same method. They may not have learned direct communication and lack problem-solving skills. When faced with potential conflict situations they resort to the PA behavior because it is all they know.

Fear of rejection. Some people are afraid that if they are direct, the other person may reject their request or even reject them. As such, PA behavior allows the person to deny responsibility if confronted perhaps even placing the blame on the other person: "I didn't mean that—you misunderstood."

Fear of anger. Some people are fearful of anger. Some may be afraid of others' anger because they have been hurt in the past. Others may be afraid of their own anger because they don't want to hurt others. Either way it results in avoidance by using PA behavior instead of directly expressing anger.

Types of Unintentional Passive-Aggressive Behavior

The hallmark of PA behavior is the communication of anger in an indirect or passive manner. When anger is not expressed directly, it is difficult to solve problems. The indirect expression of anger means that the recipient may pick up on non-verbal behavior cues indicating there is a problem but if they try to address it they are roadblocked by the following types of behavior. The PA person may be a combination of these types but usually has a preferred style.

Silent type

Instead of responding when someone confronts you, you remain silent. People who are silent when angry often are trying to avoid conflict. However, their silence indicates that a problem exists. Such behavior causes the other person to be frustrated and angry when they are trying to solve the problem.

Hinting type

This type drops hints if they are angry or want something. If the other person doesn't get their hints, they pout or become angry. Hints may seem obvious to the person doing the hinting but they are not a clear method of communicating. The problem occurs when the person believes that their hints are perfectly understandable. I've often had clients who said that they clearly told their spouse what they wanted but when I asked for the exact wording I would classify it as a hint. It is certainly not fair to the other person when you hint but think that you are communicating clearly because then the tendency is to believe the other person is deliberately ignoring you.

Denying type

This type denies feelings of anger while slamming doors or other nonverbal behaviors that show anger. However, when someone accuses you of being angry or upset, you deny it: "Nothing's wrong." A great deal of communication is facial expressions and other nonverbal behaviors. So it can be very frustrating to the other person when you deny your obvious anger. Once again, it prevents problem resolution.

Pleasing type

When angry, this type ignores their own needs and tries to please others. However, people who are pleasers frequently become resentful when others don't focus on their needs: "I'm always taking care of everyone else. How come I don't ever get anything in return?" The answer to this question is usually that other people aren't aware of the pleaser's needs or anger because the people-pleaser doesn't share that information.

Avoiding type

Instead of addressing a problem or dealing with a difficult person this type pretends there isn't a problem. Although this type is similar to the denying type, a major difference is that the denying type shows behavior indicating anger whereas the avoiding type doesn't provide any indication of anger. In fact, the topics may be avoided so completely that the avoider doesn't even know the degree of anger they feel.

Sarcastic type

Sarcasm is another type of denial. This type makes their feelings known through sarcasm but denies it if someone takes them seriously. Sarcasm is another way of avoiding a direct expression of emotions and taking responsibility for those feelings.

Anxious type

Some people with anxiety want others to behave in certain ways because of their own anxiety but instead of being direct they use indirect communication such as guilting to control them.

Accusing type

Instead of saying when they are angry or don't want to do something this type accuses the other person indirectly and with a tone: "I will take care of it just like I always do."

Nice type

This type wants to control others' decisions without appearing to control. For instance, a woman who is frustrated because her husband won't take care of his health sweetly asks, "Honey, are you sure that is what is best for you? Have you thought this through?" If confronted they are likely to deny control and indicate they are just concerned.

These are some of the unintentional ways that people can be PA. As you see, most are due to people having certain desires but instead of expressing them directly, they use indirect communication.

The above descriptions are not to diagnose someone else but to understand yourself. The problem with diagnosing someone else is that we don't always know what their underlying intention is. And PA behavior always has to do with intention: it is the indirect expression of anger. So, for instance, just because someone is procrastinating and it causes you frustration, it doesn't mean they are passive-aggressively trying to cause you frustration—they could just be procrastinating. In other words, it is not the effect on the recipient that determines passive-aggressive behavior, it is the intent of the behavior that determines it.

How Can You Change?

Choice. First, recognize that PA behavior is your choice. Just because it is how you have always behaved doesn't mean you have to continue. By looking at your communication and the consequences you can determine if PA behavior is involved. If PA behavior is causing problems or a deterioration of your relationships, you can choose to learn a more direct communication method.

Learn communication skills. Primarily, you want to learn how to communicate directly when you are angry, frustrated, resentful and need to solve an interpersonal problem. There are plenty of opportunities to learn these skills including books, seminars/classes, or even individual therapy. Excel At Life provides some articles on conflict resolution that can help you get started.

Practice. Determine some situations in which you are typically PA. Then, using what you learned about communication develop some ways of acting that are more direct and assertive. You might even write down example responses so you are more likely to remember them. It is easiest to start with situations that occur frequently because you can prepare in advance and practice (in your head or in front of a mirror) before they occur. By practicing the common situations, you will become more prepared for the less common ones.

Let others know. Tell your close friends and family that you recognize you can be PA and you are trying to work on it. However, it is a strong behavior pattern and you are not always aware of it. They can be helpful by gently letting you know when your behavior is hurtful. This step can be particularly difficult because PA people do not like being told when they are hurting someone. However, it is important to your recovery from this behavior to take responsibility for it.

Don't give up! Changing behavior takes effort. One of the more difficult aspects is that other people may still respond to you as if you are being PA. For instance, if a sarcastic person is trying to be genuine, they may still be accused of being sarcastic. Or, if a controlling person is expressing a feeling without an expectation of trying to control, that expression may still be seen by others as attempts at control. Recognize that even when you are making an effort it can be a while before you see the results of improved relationships.

Examples of Handling Passive-aggressive Behavior

The following are examples from website readers of passive-aggressive encounters they have experienced. Keep in mind that the suggested responses are not personal advice as a full evaluation of the situation is not available. As such, the suggestions may not work in every situation but are to give you an idea of possible ways to respond.

Passive-aggressive Example 1 Back-stabbing

Back-stabbing behavior often uses techniques such as hitting below the belt by using previously confided or sensitive information against the person or by communicating through someone else but with plausible deniability. This individual may even resort to showing artificial concern as a way of validating their behavior "You know I wouldn't want to hurt you but I'm only saying this because I'm concerned about you."

The co-worker who casually brings the boss's attention to mistakes:

Co-worker: I'm concerned about Sally. She must have been a little distracted yesterday when she was sending out those notices to the clients because the calculations were wrong and could really cause the company some problems. Do you think everything is okay with her? However, fortunately I caught the error early so don't worry about it.

The boss confronts Sally who tries to explain that she discovered the error when she was doing her routine checking for errors and it was in no danger of being sent to clients. However, the boss's perception of the event has already been biased due to the co-worker's seemingly caring and concerned comments. This is a no-win situation for Sally because the co-worker has malicious intentions and a confrontation would only be twisted to her own purposes such as "Sally has been so touchy and irritable lately."

Unfortunately, this type of person may be fairly skilled at influencing others. In this situation, Sally may need to clearly document everything she does so that she has evidence that opposes the co-workers comments. Depending upon the situation, she may also make the suggestion to the boss that the co-worker is overly focused on Sally's work.

The co-worker who deliberately sabotages your work:

An internet reader described the following situation: I work in a special needs preschool and I do circletime everyday. When I was sick, I asked my co-teacher aide if she will do it for me and she said "Yes." I leave to go to the restroom and return to see the head teacher doing circletime. The co-worker never says a word about why she didn't do it. Also, she has deleted pictures used to document learning and when I restored them, she permanently deleted them and denied it ever happened.

This reader gives a number of other examples, including behavior towards the special needs children, and states: I feel guilty telling on her but am about to quit my job.

This is an unfortunate example of someone deliberately trying to create problems for others. In this situation, the reader would not be able to directly confront her (in fact, it seems that she has) because the aide would only deny it. However, the key to the problem is that the reader states "I feel guilty telling on her, but am about to quit my job." This sentiment is what allows the aide to get away with her behavior--she can count on not having to be responsible for her behavior. This reader needs to deal with her irrational feelings of guilt and recognize that guilt is about doing something wrong. If she reports the aide's behavior, not only is she not doing anything wrong but she is protecting these vulnerable children from a malicious person.

I would suspect that the head teacher already has some awareness of her behavior and may just need some supporting documentation to do something about it. Whether or not she quits her job, this reader should provide the head teacher with the necessary information so that the children can be protected.

Now, this situation would be more complicated if the aide had a special or close relationship with the head teacher. In that sort of situation, the reader may need to very detailed in her documentation and may have to go above the head teacher, if reporting to the head teacher doesn't change the situation.

These back-stabbing situations are very difficult to deal with because they are usually the malicious type of passive-aggressive person. It is understandable that this reader wants to get away from this person. However, it is important to for her to see if the situation can be remedied, because I'm sure this is not the only malicious person she will have to deal with in her life. So she needs to resolve her own feelings of guilt in order to handle the situation.

Passive-aggressive Example 2 Blaming

The skilled passive-aggressive blamer can rephrase almost any comment to make it appear the recipient's fault. "You should have known!" or "You're too sensitive!" are common methods of blaming the victim. Sometimes it can be so extreme as to border on the ridiculous if it wasn't so hurtful; for example, "You know I'm a grouch before dinner. I wouldn't have yelled at you if you wouldn't have asked me a question." This person deflects all attempts to communicate about problems by blaming the other person.

The husband who deflects issues by counter-attacking:

Wife: I'm concerned about how much your spending on your fishing trips. Can we talk about this?

Husband: You're really one to talk! Look at the credit card records and see how much you spent at the department stores.

Wife: If you are concerned about that we can discuss it, but right now I'd like to talk about these expenses for your fishing trips.

Husband: All you ever do is nag me about how much I spend! If you didn't nag me all the time I wouldn't be out fishing so much!

Wife: I'm not nagging you! I'm trying to discuss something that worries me!

Husband: See! You are always worrying about every little thing.

Wife: I don't think the things I worry about are "little."

As you see in this example, even though the wife is trying to reasonably focus on a concern, the husband continues to blame her and to deflect the issue away from his spending and onto his wife. He has successfully shifted the argument so that the wife is defending herself at which point he has "won" because he no longer has to discuss his spending behavior.

Passive-aggressive Example 3 Controlling

Controlling behavior seeks to control the individual in an indirect manner. For instance, a man who emotionally abuses his partner says "No one could ever love you the way I do" with the intended result being insecurity in the woman so that she won't leave him. Another example is parents telling their adult children that they should respect or love them because they are their parents thus trying to control their behavior. Love and respect is something that occurs due to the underlying relationship not because of a demand.

An adolescent trying to control a parent's emotional responses:

Mother: Hurry up. We're going to be late for school.

Daughter ignores the demand and obviously slows down her movements

Mother: Stop trying to irritate me! We need to leave soon.

Daughter: I'm not doing anything.

Mother: I can see you slowing down when I tell you to hurry.

Daughter: You're imagining that. All you want to do is yell at me.

Mother: I've had it with you! You are such a brat!

Daughter (crying now): See, all you do is yell at me and call me names!

In this scenario the daughter is in control and has caused her mother to lose control. Instead of trying to control the daughter (which ultimately allows the daughter control over her) she should determine natural or logical consequences for the behavior and allow the daughter to have to deal with the consequences. For instance, some schools give detentions if a child is late for class in which case the mother doesn't need to do anything. In fact, it's best in the case of the natural consequences to just ignore the child's passive-aggressive behavior (slowing down) and just let the consequences occur with no comment. Not even "I told you."

Passive-aggressive Example 4 Denial

The denial type of passive-aggressive behavior occurs when the individual appears to be distressed, frustrated, bored, confused, or any number of emotions but when questioned refuses to admit to the feeling. They may outright deny or they may avoid by ignoring, working, or deflecting with humor. However, the behavior has the outcome of frustrating the recipient because they are unable to confront and resolve the problem. Thus, this individual is able to control the other by not engaging in conflict resolution when an obvious problem has occurred.

The wife who expects her husband to read her mind:

Husband: Is everything okay?

Wife: Of course everything is okay. Why wouldn't it be? (with sarcastic tone)

Husband (who doesn't know how to interpret sarcastic tone):Okay, you just seemed quiet. Anyway like I said, I'm going out with the guys tonight.

Wife (walks away in a huff)

In this example the husband can only interpret the wife's words. She's angry because he doesn't know that she is upset because he is spending the evening with friends. However, she said everything is "okay" and he doesn't pursue it further. The problem with the wife's behavior is that many men do not easily understand emotional content of a message especially when the verbal content is the opposite. This creates a cognitive dissonance (an internal emotional conflict) which is resolved by focusing on the verbal content and ignoring the opposing emotional content. This is not done deliberately but is the way the man's brain reacts to such conflict.

Unfortunately, many women are the opposite and focus on the emotional content and ignore the verbal content if the two are in conflict. These women also expect the men in their lives to do the same and often believe that he is deliberately ignoring their "obvious" emotional messages. This particular type of unintentional passive-aggressive behavior creates many problems in relationships.

Passive-aggressive Example 5 Guilting

Guilting behavior controls through using guilt either directly or indirectly to control the other. An indirect form of guilt may be "Don't worry about me...I'll be okay" followed by a sigh. A more direct form may be describing all the efforts made on your behalf followed by an expectation "I've only cleaned the house today, taken the kids to their activities, checked on your mom. Taking me out to dinner isn't too much to ask, is it?"

Father of adult child wanting him to visit his mother more:

Son: But, Dad, I call Mom everyday to see how she's doing.

Father: I know, but she's just so lonely and it means so much to her when you visit.

Son: I don't have a lot of time lately.

Father: Well I'm not sure how much time your mother has left.

You can certainly see how the son can't win this one. With guilt-inducing passive-aggressive behavior it is more important to address the underlying cognitions or "shoulds" about the behavior. You can only be made to feel guilty if you believe that you "should" engage in the behavior. In this example, if the son believes he is neglectful if he doesn't visit more often, then he is more likely to be controlled by these comments. However, if he believes that he is doing the best he can do given the circumstances of his life, then he is not likely to feel guilty and can respond with the broken-record technique:

Father: Your mother wouldn't say anything herself but I think she feels like you don't care about her.

Son: I'm doing the best I can.

Father: I know, but she's just so lonely and it means so much to her when you visit.

Son: I'm doing the best I can.

Father: Well I'm not sure how much time your mother has left.

Son: I'm doing the best I can.

Passive-aggressive Example 6 Wife's Withholding and Denial

Question: My wife and I are having serious issues. She says I am angry all the time. I tell her I am not angry, just angry at her. She denies her actions causes issues in our marriage.

Examples:

> 1. Every year I asked to go to Vegas. She says Vegas seems dirty and doesn't want to go. When I get home from Afghanistan she goes to Vegas with her friends. When I get upset she makes me feel like I was being stupid and selfish.

> 2. When I returned home she would make comments on how it was nice to have the entire bed to herself to stretch out.

> 3. When we went to counseling I expressed she spends too much time hanging out with her friends. One hour after we get back from counseling she asks if she can hang out with her friends.

> 4. I asked her to help clean the house. She doesn't clean. I then say if you don't want to clean get a maid. After 4 years I finally got a maid myself.

> 5. She asked what I want for my birthday. I told her but a year later I am still waiting.

> 6. The new thing is now she is withholding intimacy.

Response: The above description of the wife's behavior indicates there are serious problems in this relationship. However, the passive-aggressive (PA) behavior deflects the issues onto the husband's anger rather than resolving the problems in the marriage. The husband wrote that he is having serious issues with his wife who accuses him of being angry all the time. He indicates that he is angry with her behavior, but she denies that her behavior is a problem. This may be classic PA denial which has the effect of creating anger in the victim. However, this is a good example of how it does no good to complain or become angry because the PA person has then "won" the conflict by displacing it onto the victim (husband) and causing him to look unreasonable. It also is not effective to take an article such as this one and tell her to read it because that will only escalate conflict. It is best to address each issue as it occurs, but to address it with a deeper emotion rather than anger. The anger only justifies the PA person's behavior such as the wife's response: "You have an anger problem."

This reader wrote that he wanted to visit Vegas and his wife didn't want to, but then went with her friends. When he became "upset" she made him feel "stupid and selfish." Anger is a protective emotion which is an outer layer emotion. The deeper emotion, or inner layer, is probably hurt or disappointment or fear. So, it would be better to respond with an assertive statement such as "I feel afraid that you don't love me anymore (or you find me boring) when you would rather go to Vegas with your friends than with me." This way he avoids the accusation of being angry and has the opportunity of her responding with something other than "You're angry all the time."

Another example this reader provided was that when he returned home from overseas, she commented about how nice it was to have the entire bed to herself. Again, he could respond assertively by saying, "I feel disappointed that you don't seem happy to share the bed with me." Notice the assertive statements use the "I" statements where you begin with your emotion and then follow it with the problem behavior or feeling. This type of assertive statement gently confronts the comments rather than immediately believing that his assumptions are correct (and becoming angry). For instance, it is possible that the comment wasn't about him but about how the bed is more comfortable when she is alone.

Ideally, it would be nice if the PA person could recognize her problem and try to be more direct about what she is feeling and what the problems are. However, in the case of a denier that is not likely, so he needs to change the angry response. It is possible that if he quits responding to her passive-aggressiveness with anger, they will be able to address the real problems in their relationship especially since they are already receiving therapeutic help.

Passive-aggressive Example 7 Boyfriend's Critical Roommate

Question: My boyfriend's roommate is overly critical of every statement I make and brings negativity to my ideas. I think this is because he thinks we spend too much time together, but also because I think he hates women. He is trying to make me feel as uncomfortable as possible so that I will stop coming to a place where I am made to feel bad. Regardless, I'm not going to stop seeing my boyfriend, but how do I respond to his passive-aggressive comments?

Response: This is a good example of not only passive-aggressive (PA) behavior but making assumptions about someone else's behavior. Now, certainly, it is possible that the girlfriend is able to "read" the roommate's intentions and personality, but frequently assumptions are wrong. For example, instead of the roommate hating women, perhaps he is uncomfortable with women or doesn't know how to treat them. Therefore, a technique that can potentially defuse the PA behavior as well as uncover more about the roommate's intentions is best used in this situation.

For example, the girlfriend could show an interest in the roommate's comments. In an inquiring way (with an innocent, not accusing tone) she could ask, "Oh, what makes you think that?" or "How do you think I could do that better?" If the roommate is truly being PA such non-defensive statements would throw him off his game. PA people want to irritate or escalate without having to take responsibility for their behavior. This type of inquiry places the responsibility for his statements on the roommate but in a non-defensive, non-hostile manner. If the girlfriend continues this type of gentle prodding every time, he will likely discontinue the comments if he is truly PA because PA people do not want to explain their comments—it defeats the purpose of a sneak attack.

However, if the roommate is not being passive-aggressive, but there is some other reason for his behavior, such an inquiry can possibly gain more information. The girlfriend may be able to establish a better understanding of his intention and comments.

Passive-aggressive Example 8 Mother-in-law and Communication Problems

Question: My soon to be mother-in-law texted me about the camping menu for the next weekend hunt. I knew she had left out the other son's girlfriend ("Sue") before so I suggested she text Sue and see what she was thinking of making. My mother-in-law did not know I had already talked to Sue who said she wanted cereal and soup, easy and cheap. I never got a call back so I thought that was what we were going to do. We were the last ones to the camp. They had made two dutch ovens with casseroles in them! We had stopped at the last gas station for something before we headed out of town and got something cheap. So when she had changed Sue's meal plans to big dinners and french toast in the morning my boyfriend saw how hurt I was and told his mom we need better communication about food planning. She wouldn't even look at us and said "we knew we had plenty for everyone." Then she said Dad can't even eat soup. Then why wouldn't she have told me that earlier in the week? I started crying and went to the truck. What am I dealing with? She never says what she really means. We just got home from camp and I sent her a text saying " I know you didn't mean to hurt my feelings by not calling me back about the meal planning, but if you can please text me what I need to bring next week so I'm prepared and not left out of the loop, I'm going to the store soon." She sent back what to bring but not a word to answer me about hurting my feelings. I am VERY direct and have a leadership type personality with a bit of a people-pleaser in me so I don't know what to do when she says "well we knew we had enough for everyone." What do I do? I need to handle this before I marry her son.

Response: Given just the information provided here it is not clear whether the mother-in-law is passive-aggressive (PA) or is a poor communicator. Generally, it is best to make the most benign interpretation of someone's behavior until proven otherwise. However, this daughter-in-law may have more information other than this one instance to make her judgments.

If this is truly PA behavior, one thing to keep in mind is that PA people can only affect you to the degree that you give them control over you. The more important an outcome is to you, the more opportunity the PA person has to hurt you. So, the question here is: why were the daughter-in-law's feelings hurt? The writer says that she is a people-pleaser so my assumption is that she was unable to engage in her people-pleasing behavior (being a good daughter-in-law and contributing to the family event) as a result of the mother-in-law's PA behavior or poor communication.

However, that is the writer's issue, not the mother-in-law's. What I mean by this is that if she was not trying to please anyone, instead of getting her feelings hurt she could have responded with "Oh, that was so nice of you to take care of the meals. Please let me know next time what the plan is so I can contribute, too." Notice the wording with this. It really doesn't matter whether the mother-in-law is PA or just a poor communicator. This response confronts the behavior in a gentle way but places the responsibility on the mother-in-law for future situations. This is especially important for a people-pleaser who most likely tends to take too much responsibility.

Confronting gently is important for two reasons. One, if the mother-in-law's behavior is poor communication, it won't confuse and escalate the situation. Two, if the mother-in-law is PA, it won't reinforce the PA behavior by rewarding it. People who are PA want to attack without having to be responsible for their behavior. If the daughter-in-law directly confronts the behavior, the PA person is likely to respond "You are just too sensitive" or "You are making a big deal out of nothing."

Another problem with this incident is the daughter-in-law's texting her mother-in-law about her hurt feelings rather than discussing the problem face-to-face. This is an issue that is becoming all too common with the advent of new technology such as texting. In my opinion, although people are communicating more, the quality of communication has become much worse.

Non-verbals are an important part of communication especially when discussing emotions. Under the best of circumstances it is easy to misunderstand emotions, and texting is not the best of circumstances. I don't believe that it is ever a good idea to communicate emotions through texting. Frequently, my clients have read me texts that they claimed were critical or demanding or hurtful, yet when I read the texts back with a different tone they agreed that maybe the text had a different meaning. No matter how many emoticons are used with texting, tone of voice and other non-verbals can never be accurately communicated by text.

The daughter-in-law had an expectation that the mother-in-law would respond to her "texted" feelings of being hurt but she did not ask the mother-in-law to address the issue. In fact, the mother-in-law addressed exactly what she asked "please text me what I need to bring." But the daughter-in-law is upset because the mother-in-law did not read her mind and know that she wanted a response to her hurt feelings. Unless there was more communication regarding this that we are unaware of, how was the mother-in-law to know?

Another mistake made by the daughter-in-law was the assumption that what she had discussed with Sue was the final decision. Again, there was a breakdown in communication. It was as much her responsibility as her mother-in-law's to determine what was the final outcome. If my assumption that as a people-pleaser she tends to take too much responsibility is accurate, it is also possible that she has an expectation that others will take the same amount of responsibility as her. Such an expectation can easily lead to assumptions and misunderstandings.

Finally, if the mother-in-law is truly PA, then it is best for feelings to be stated at the time that the feelings were hurt, "I feel left out because you didn't tell me the meal plans were changed. I am embarrassed that we didn't contribute." Notice that the reasons for the emotions are very specific which is critical to clear communication. By expressing hurt feelings clearly and directly it is likely to decrease future PA behavior because the PA person knows that she will be confronted and have to be responsible for her actions.

I know in this situation I'm pointing out the problems in the daughter-in-law's communication and assumptions. However, this is a critical point regarding dealing with PA behavior. It is first important to make sure that you are understanding the behavior accurately and that your communication is assertive. Once you are certain of that, the PA behavior of others becomes more clear. This situation, as described, is not clear, which indicates the daughter-in-law needs to address her responses prior to making assumptions about the mother-in-law.

Passive-aggressive Example 9 Siblings Won't Help with Elderly Father

Question: I am fourth in a family of 5 siblings. Our elderly father is now 93 and still living on his own, primarily because I drive 200 miles each weekend to take care of a host of things for him. I've repeatedly tried to get my other siblings involved, but they ignore me. It is no more difficult for them to participate than me, yet they repeatedly just ignore me. Often I send an email asking if they'll visit on a holiday, or mentioning there's a problem with something in the house. And still, no response. I've been doing this for minimally 10 years. Even though I see the others maybe once a year, they never address this glaring issue and if I bring it up, they immediately leave or act as though I have some big emotional problem. A friend who is a psychologist, categorized this behavior as passive-aggressive. Is this true ? I did not find something that rang true in the list of behaviors at the website. I'm trying to understand the behavior, and find tools to deal with it all more effectively.

Response: Certainly, the aspect of this situation where the siblings won't address the problem directly but act as if she has a "big emotional problem" is passive-aggressive behavior (specifically blaming). The purpose of this behavior is to deflect an issue they don't want to face. By making her the "bad guy" they don't have to acknowledge the problem or their behavior. They don't have to say "I don't care about Dad" or "I don't want to help." Obviously, acknowledging those things would make them look bad, so they protect their self-image by making the writer out to be the "emotional" or "crazy" one.

However, there is another issue here and that is the writer has been doing this for 10 years! It is time for her to recognize that they are not going to help. Part of her stress comes from beating her head against the wall that her siblings have created. By recognizing that she can't expect them to help, she can then move on to other decisions. "Knowing that my siblings aren't going to help, how do I best manage this situation? How can I take care of myself while taking care of Dad? What assistance is available to help with an elderly parent?" She can also decide what kind of relationship she wants to have with her siblings by recognizing their limitations and whether she can accept those limitations are not. But she cannot make them change or care—10 years is proof of that!

Passive-aggressive Example 10 Mother's "Helpful" Criticism

Question: Mother upon seeing outfit daughter was wearing to work: You know why Hillary Clinton wears pants? Because she has those cankles, right? She is smart. (pause) You shouldn't wear your skirts that short either. You can't help it if you are built like your grandmother but you should wear your skirts longer to cover more of your legs. I am only trying to HELP you since you look very nice but you would look better if you wore your dresses longer...

Daughter: Are you saying I have cankles MA??

Mother: NO! Where do you get this stuff? I was only pointing out that you have legs like your grandmother and you can't help it if they are sorta bowed..

Daughter: I DO NOT HAVE BOWED LEGS MA!!! AND I DON"T HAVE CANKLES EITHER!!

Mother: No one said you did - where do you get this? You are constantly over-reacting! I was only pointing out that you look better in longer length skirts!

Response: This is a classic passive-aggressive (PA) example because it shows the escalation, blame, and denial. As I indicated in the "Crazy-Makers" article, the purpose of PA behavior is to attack without having to be responsible. In fact, this example uses the all-too-common "I am only trying to help" which is not only denying responsibility but attempting to appear benevolent which sets the daughter up for the final attack of "you are over-reacting." In other words, the guilt-inducing message is "All I'm doing is trying to help you and you are just unreasonable."

So we have the sequence of events starting with criticism disguised as help, denial when confronted regarding the criticism, an escalation of emotions by the victim of the attack, and finally, blaming the victim. This type of PA attacker is very skilled so that any confrontation can be deflected back and blamed on the victim.

Therefore, it is important for the daughter to remain calm. As soon as she starts to respond to the criticism and argue back, the mother has achieved her purpose which is to criticize but not have to be responsible for being hurtful. Once the daughter becomes emotional, the mother can place the blame for the conflict on her.

In addition, the daughter needs to keep in mind that she can't change her mother's behavior but that she has control of her own. The only way her mother doesn't win this conflict is if the daughter doesn't get emotionally involved. However, that doesn't mean she can't express her emotions. It just means that it needs to be done in a way that places the responsibility with her mother.

For example:

Daughter: It hurts my feelings when you criticize my outfit.

Mother: I'm just trying to help!

Daughter: I'm letting you know that the way you are trying to help hurts my feelings.

Mother: You are just over-reacting!

Daughter: I may be over-reacting but I'm letting you know that you are hurting me. So if you continue, I will assume that is your intention.

If the mother still doesn't stop, the daughter can set a consequence. For example, she can refuse to continue to talking about it (but do this calmly): "I will not discuss this any further."

If this is done calmly and repeatedly whenever the mother makes such comments, it is likely to reduce the comments because it confronts the mother in a way that doesn't allow her to retreat as easily behind denial and blame.

Notice that I'm using several techniques in this response. One technique is ignoring the bait and not becoming emotional. The second technique is using a broken record of repetition "You are hurting me." The third technique is agreeing rather than arguing: "I may be over-reacting." This last technique is particularly useful when the PA person wants to start an argument and then blame the victim. So the technique is to agree so as not to become distracted from your point: "You are hurting me."

By the way, direct confrontation of the behavior such as telling the PA person that they are PA will only escalate the conflict which the PA person is almost always sure to win. It is best to take an approach as described above and be consistent.

Passive-aggressive Example 11 Co-worker's "Joking" Criticism

Question: My coworker has on five occasions commented on me never being at the office. I work at home one or two days a week as do others. However, he seems to want to point out that I'm never at the office. It always seems to be a joke. For example: I would compliment him on his attire and he would say "I always dress like this. You would know if you were here." Not sure what to say back to him....help?!!

Response: This is a good example of a passive-aggressive way of making an indirect criticism and causing defensiveness in the other person. However, as indicated in the article "Crazy-Makers", the purpose of passive-aggressive behavior is to create a reaction without having to be responsible. So, in this instance, if the woman would respond defensively, "I have permission to work from home" he would know he had achieved his goal of creating a reaction but would deny responsibility by stating something like "I was just teasing you." If she were to be more direct and say "Stop hassling me about working from home" he would somehow place the blame on her "Wow! Aren't you sensitive? I didn't mean anything by it."

The best response to this situation is for her to be non-defensive as if she didn't even hear the underlying criticism. For example, she could respond with a laugh, "Yes, isn't it great that I don't have to be here everyday?!" In this way, his attempt to irritate and create a reaction is undercut. As a result, he doesn't achieve his goal and he is less likely to continue especially if she continues to respond in the same way to his passive-aggressive comments.

Passive-aggressive Example 12 Husband's Passive Aggressive Avoidance

Question:

Wife: "I really need to move from where we live now."

Husband: "We can't afford it."

Wife: "True, but if you found a well-paying job in the new location, we could improve our income."

Husband: "So start looking for a school for the kids in the new location".

Wife inquires and looks for school in new location, finds school, makes appointment for daughter for entrance exam, takes daughter for entrance exam, follows up with phone calls, makes appointment for interview and takes daughter for interview.

Wife: "How's it going with looking for a job in new location?"

Husband: "I phoned up one place, there was no reply. What are you doing about schools for the kids?"

Wife: "I feel I've done enough for the time being, I'm waiting to see developments from your end."

Husband: "See? You're not prepared to do anything to make the move work so I'm not going to do any more either!"

Response: This is an example where I would refer the reader to my article "Why Are People Mean?" because it is probably not malicious passive-aggressive behavior but due to some other issue and so it may be an avoidance of that other issue. But the avoidance comes across as passive-aggressive. In which case, it may be important to try and determine what is the underlying issue. I would suggest that in a calm, supportive and understanding way the wife should try to approach the subject and find out what the issue may be. For example, "I know this can be a big step to take and change can be difficult. But I'm here to support you. Is there something that is holding you back from making the move? Are you worried about taking this step? What can I do to help you?" Hopefully, the husband will be able to share more of his concerns if he's not feeling pressure, but support. Then the two of them can have a conversation focused on resolving those concerns.

WIFE'S COMMENTS TO MY RESPONSE:

Actually, the example I gave comes from someone who is clearly passive-aggressive so in this case there may not be much to argue about.

Here's another example:

Husband is sitting in middle of table, wife at the end of table with child on her lap.

Wife: "Pass the pitcher please."

Husband: "You can get it yourself, if you try."

In this case, the wife realized the futility of continuing the discussion, requested from child to get off her lap for a moment, stood up, reached out and took the pitcher herself.

Later in a quiet moment,

Wife: "Why weren't you willing to pass me the pitcher?"

Husband: "Because you never do anything yourself, you just sit around and expect everyone else to serve your needs."

This actually developed into a long discussion about the wife's needs, etc. until the husband very surprisingly came to the conclusion, "Do you mean to say that if I improved my attitude things would be better?" WOW! after 21 years, maybe we've made some progress, thank God. Now all that we need to do is for him to actually see the progress if he improves his attitude--obviously, if he doesn't see any improvement in wife's attitude towards him, it will be her fault. So, wife is going to have to take this to heart and be extra nice when he improves.

Response:The wife is making an excellent point here. Her husband uses passive-aggressive blame in order to avoid things that are unpleasant or uncomfortable for him. However, if he makes even a tiny bit of progress with his attitude, she needs to reward that progress through her response to him. The best way to increase desirable behavior is to reinforce it, not criticize the undesirable behavior. In this situation, since they have had what I call "the talk," she can now focus on watching for even small increments of change and reinforcing them.

Passive-aggressive Example 13 Volunteer Using to Control

Question: We have a volunteer who behaves like she's in charge. She sends out messages on behalf of the organization (of which she's not actually a full member). If given an opportunity she'll change decisions that have been made previously. She ingratiates herself with members so she can be defended. She incites anger and then sends wounded messages to certain people in the organization. People are complaining about her and I worry we'll lose real members if we cannot get rid of her.

Response: In response to this writer, I will make several assumptions: 1) the volunteer has made friends with people in the organization who protect her; 2) the anger she incites is among the staff running the organization, not the membership; and 3) the writer does not have the authority to fire her. (To the writer: If any of these assumptions are wrong, let me know).

The behavior described appears to be a passive-aggressive (PA) controlling style. The volunteer is able to maintain her position by controlling the responses of others. The best place to start with managing this volunteer is to not respond with anger. This may require some staff training so that everyone can provide a consistent response. The problem with confronting PA with anger is that the staff is now playing her game and she has won if she can run "wounded" to powerful others who then play the part of her defenders.

Instead, there needs to be a single person to whom the staff can turn who can directly confront each and every instance of inappropriate behavior. As I've indicated elsewhere PA people hate being confronted about their behavior. In this case, this volunteer has the agenda of achieving control in an indirect manner so that she can deny that she is doing anything wrong, and that instead, she is the victim.

However, confronting her requires a calm and direct approach with a focus on specific behaviors, not overall intentions. Do NOT, for instance, say "You are destroying this organization" or "You are creating problems." These statements are accusations that are too general and she'll play the victim.

Instead, make statements such as "Sending this message without clearance has confused members of the organization. You need to send out a correction stating that you acted without authority." Notice that this statement not only confronts without angry accusations, but it also provides a consequence to her behavior. If she refuses, send out the correction anyway (but in a straight-forward, non-accusing way). By doing so, it may allow those who are defending her to see her actual behavior instead of her self-reported victimization.

Passive-aggressive Example 14 Sister's Lack of Support

Question: I've had to work at different locations due to personal conflict with my boss. At the beginning of this saga, I stated to my sister who works for the same company "I'll never work for that boss again." Well, after a year of drama, it looks like I will be going back to that location. I feel like my sister is trying to rub my nose in it. She left a long-winded message on the phone about me returning and told my mother about it. I feel irritated by it. What should I do?

Response: Obviously, we aren't privy to the tone of the sister's comments, but according to the writer's description we can assume the tone is either sarcastic or somewhat gleeful such as "I guess you're going back after all." In that case, this would be an example of back-stabbing passive-aggressive behavior (PA) because when the writer needs her support, the sister uses sensitive information against her.

This is a case where it might be best to directly confront the PA behavior. However, it needs to be done with a careful attention to the wording so that it is not accusatory. For instance, she could say to the sister "I'm sure this wasn't your intention but it sounds as if you are happy that I have to return to a miserable situation." This type of statement puts the sister in a bind because she certainly can't admit she is happy about it (unless she is truly malicious which is then an entirely different issue) so she is more likely to respond with support: "Oh, no, I didn't mean it that way. I'm just worried about you."

Some people reading this might think that's not a true show of support. However, it is, because if we confront someone's behavior and they care enough to change, then it is meaningful. In this case, we don't know why the sister acted this way, but if she is given the benefit of the doubt maybe the relationship can improve. The important part of confronting as suggested is that it helps the writer determine if the behavior is malicious or not (based on the sister's response). If it is malicious and meant to intentionally hurt, the writer may need to re-think her relationship with her sister.

Passive-aggressive Example 15 Grandmother's Criticism of Child

Question: My mother criticizes my 10-year-old son about his hair, clothes, the activities he likes, you name it. He's a good kid, does well in school, and I think that he should be able to make his own choices about these things. I can see that my son is hurt by this criticism. When I try to tell my mother to stop, she and my sister say, "He's a boy and he needs to toughen up. He needs to be able to handle teasing. You're just over-protecting him." Is she right? How do I get her to stop?

Response: This is a case where a passive-aggressive (PA) justification is used for the criticism that the grandmother dishes out. The type of PA behavior used here is a combination of denial and blame. This mother has probably been subjected to this PA behavior all her life as evidenced by her self-doubting question: "Is she right?" This type of PA behavior often makes the recipient question her own perspective because the PA person is often very strong in her insistence that her view is correct.

This situation is potentially damaging to the child. It is important that the child understand that his mother will protect him and that he does not need to passively tolerate unacceptable behavior from others. Therefore, the mother needs to take stronger steps than trying to tell her mother to stop. She needs to ignore the mother's denial and blame and set consequences. She may not have control over her mother's behavior but she does have control over herself and her decisions regarding her son.

What she can do is make a demand rather than a request "Stop being critical of my son." It is okay to do this in her son's presense so that he knows his grandmother's behavior is not appropriate and that he is not bad or wrong. When the grandmother responds with her usual PA statements, the mother needs to tell her "This criticism is not acceptable. If you do not stop, we will be leaving." She should not get in a discussion about it. The only two acceptable outcomes is that the grandmother stops or she and her son leave.

This may or may not impact the grandmother's behavior but it does protect the son. However, I have seen numerous cases where the grandmother's behavior did eventually change as long as the daughter continued to set the limits.

Passive-aggressive Example 16 Disrespectful Attitude from Adult Child

Question: I am the mother of a 36-year-old daughter. Our relationship is very strained. She repeatedly speaks to me with sarcastic intonations in spite of my numerous requests for her to "try to talk nice." She rolls her eyes and smirks at me openly. Then when I get upset/hurt, she says I'm making a big deal about nothing and tells me I drive her crazy. When I try to put some time/distance between us so that things can cool down and I can focus on the things I need to do to take care of myself, she calls me, always due to the latest crisis with which she desperately needs my help (usually requires monetary assistance--something I have in short supply myself). I end up helping her and my son-in-law mostly in the interest of helping my grandchildren. No thank you, no sign of appreciation, and if I say anything that indicates even remotely that a little appreciation would be nice, then the sarcasm starts up, or screaming, or I get cursed out. I realize I'm a huge part of this equation, but I feel like I'm on a merry-go-round, and I don't know how to get off. I see that I am repeating/reliving my relationship with my mother (deceased) with my daughter, and it makes me sick. I feel like my heart is broken. Please help!

Response: This is a situation where both the mother and daughter are angry with one another but are unable to communicate their feelings directly. As a result, passive-aggressive (PA) behavior occurs from both sides. The daughter is using primarily sarcastic and blaming PA behavior whereas the mother is using controlling PA behavior ("...if I say anything that indicates even remotely that a little appreciation would be nice..."). This is a common problem between adult mothers and daughters because women have often been conditioned from very young to be indirect in their communication which leads to PA communication. I have divided this question up into three components on this website to illustrate how to manage situations using the tools of cognitive-behavioral therapy (CBT). The first step is education which I address in a PsychNote. The second step is examining and challenging the mother's thinking regarding the situation which I describe in a Cognitive Diary Example. And the third step is changing the response to the situation as I discuss here.

If the mother has already focused on changing her thinking about the situation she can gain a little emotional distance from the situation which can help her in deciding what would be a better response to her daughter's behavior. In particular, if you have read my article about PA behavior, the goal of the PA person is to indirectly express anger without having to take responsibility. In this situation, the daughter starts with sarcasm and facial expressions. If she is confronted it gives her the opportunity to blame the mother about being overly reactive. This then escalates into more aggressive behavior which the daughter justifies by accusing the mother of "driving her crazy."

The mother needs to remove herself from this pattern. If she has worked on her thinking she already recognizes that trying to control her adult daughter only leads to escalation. Therefore, she needs to do the opposite. She shouldn't try to get her daughter to change behavior or to express appreciation. If she doesn't appreciate the mother's help, the mother doesn't need to continue to help. The mother can use behavior rather than words to manage the situation. When the daughter treats her poorly, the mother can calmly (this is important!) leave the situation or hang up the phone. If the daughter tries to draw her into conflict by saying that she is "making a big deal about nothing" she should have a simple response such as "Maybe I am but I don't like it when you treat me this way." She should not attempt to argue or explain further.

The bottom line with this situation is simply to not engage. But for the mother to not engage she must first change her thinking regarding trying to get her daughter to behave better. Only by doing so will she be able to disengage from the situation. As I indicated, this is a good example of how the different components of CBT work together to help manage a situation.

Passive-aggressive Example 17 Sarcastic Ex

Question: I wrote a Facebook status about my part time job (cashier, retail), how I spent the day making bouquets, how fun it was and maybe I should change my part time work to Florist. I also hold a B.A. in Graphic Design and am currently in training for web design for my career. An ex who used to mock me for not finding something in my field immediately after graduation commented on my status with "I think Florist goes quite well with your degree..." When I called him out on how rude his statement was he flipped it around saying he was trying to be nice and actually serious and that I was being "so dramatic and overreacting." It made me question how I felt for a second but friends and family members with no insight to the situation fully agreed that when they saw the comment they took it as dripping with sarcasm and rude. Needless to say I messaged him directly confronting the issue. Then when he continued to place blame on me and spew more hurtful words I removed him from Facebook.

Response: This is a good example of how effective sarcastic passive-aggressive (PA) comments can be especially when there is no "sarcastic tone" as in a Facebook post or email. Although we can't be absolutely sure this comment was PA sarcasm, given the past history specifically regarding this issue it is likely that it was.

However, this is also a good example of why it doesn't matter if it is PA or not because the response could still be the same. As I've discussed before, what is the goal of the PA person? The goal is to upset you by making you mad, feel bad or crazy, or doubt yourself while being able to deny responsibility. In this instance, the PA person was successful because he created distress and conflict which he was then able to blame on her. He achieved his goal! However, in this situation she was able to satisfactorily resolve it by blocking him from Facebook so she doesn't have to continue to deal with the PA behavior and blame.

But what about a situation where you can't do that? When you have to deal with a person on a regular basis? The best type of response to such ambiguous sarcasm is one that doesn't allow the PA person to achieve his goal. When you prevent the PA person from achieving their goal, they are the one experiencing frustration rather than you. It even allows you a little PA satisfaction that you were able to turn the behavior back on them!

So, what type of response prevents the PA person in this situation from achieving his goal? Either no response or a "thank you." The no response is simple enough to do on a Facebook post. However, if this situation was more direct, a "Thank you. I think so, too" would prevent him from achieving his goal of making her feel bad and then being able to blame her. In addition, if he was actually trying to be nice, this response prevents her from appearing as if she is overreacting.

I especially like the "thank you" because it is particularly frustrating for a PA person to think that not only did he not achieve his goal but she took it as compliment. There really is no way out for him in this situation because he can't come back and say "I meant that sarcastically" without looking like the bad guy. If you continue to respond in this way to a PA person, it is likely they will discontinue the sarcasm because it not only is ineffective but it is frustrating for them.

Passive-aggressive Example 18 Boyfriend Gets Defensive

Question: I asked my boyfriend when was he planning on leaving the transitional house he's been in for 8 years. He starts asking what would be the benefit of leaving? The conversation then starts to escalate. I'm trying to explain the benefit of leaving...which is a no brainer. Then he starts to yell. I tell him to lower his voice which meant that I was yelling as well. He then says "You're yelling louder than me" and how could he get a word in when I'm talking over him? Then he storms out. The conversation did not get resolved.

Response: Although I think this writer is complaining about her boyfriend's passive-aggressive (PA) behavior, this is a good example of how PA behavior can create PA behavior in the other person. If we examine her description of the event, we can see how her initial PA behavior caused this situation to devolve into an argument rather than create a productive discussion.

Let's look at this more closely. Why am I saying her behavior is PA? When she says the benefit of leaving is a "no brainer" she is indicating she only wants one answer. She doesn't really want to have a discussion about him moving. She just wants him to do what she wants. Additionally, this indicates that she is angry with him about this issue but rather than expressing her anger appropriately it comes across as a controlling type of PA behavior. I don't know exactly what she said to him but he obviously got this message from her in some way: "I don't care about your reasons for staying, I just want you to move."

So, how can this interaction be changed? Fortunately, this is under her control because she can change her PA behavior. Instead of discussing the "benefits" of him moving, she can express how she feels. For instance, she can say "I feel frustrated because I don't understand why you won't move." By making this an "I" statement she is owning her feelings rather than making accusations about him. "You" statements such as "you should move because..." only cause the other person to become defensive which then is likely to escalate the disagreement.

The second step is instead of telling him what she thinks, she should listen, listen, listen! He apparently has some thoughts on the subject but she is "talking over him." He doesn't feel heard. Certainly, this may not get her what she wants. She may not be able to control the outcome of his decision. However, it is more likely to lead to a better relationship because it allows for greater communication. Most likely, she believes that she IS communicating because she is telling him what she thinks. However, communication also involves active listening.

What is "active" listening? It means not just waiting for the other person to finish so that you can say what you think and get him to agree with you. It means to truly listen, ask questions, and express in your own words what you think the other person is saying. "What I understand that you are saying is that you don't want to move right now because you think..." This allows the other person to more thoroughly explain his position or to correct any misunderstandings. This is what true communication is all about.

Passive-aggressive Example 19 Mother-in-law Wants to be Center of Attention

Question: My soon-to-be mother-in-law always wants to be the center of attention. The last straw is she wants to wear a dress to MY wedding that is fancier than my wedding dress! I think this is a deliberate passive-aggressive attempt to make me look bad on my wedding day. She didn't do this at her daughter's wedding! How can I stop her?

Response: What appears to be passive-aggressive may not always be passive-aggressive (PA). It is often important not to assume PA behavior. Otherwise, you will frequently find yourself angry and distressed when it may not be intentional PA behavior. Maybe this mother-in-law (MIL) wants to be the center of attention, but it seems to be an assumption to conclude "this is a deliberate passive-aggressive attempt to make me look bad."

The bride is over-reacting here for a couple of reasons. No matter what the MIL wears she is not going to get more attention than the bride (unless maybe she goes naked). If she does overdo it, she will just make herself look silly which is no reflection on the bride or the wedding. Everybody has embarrassing relatives at weddings so other people empathize and it is not going to detract from the bride's day. The more gracious the bride can be in the face of embarrassing relatives, the better she is perceived by others. This means not confronting, not getting upset, and not talking behind the MIL's back.

Secondly, assumptions are dangerous and can have a cascading negative effect on what is going to be a long-term relationship with the MIL. If she continues to be angry, it is likely to lead to confrontation or retaliatory PA behavior on the part of the bride which will only lead to a deterioration of the relationship. It is up to the bride to determine how she wants this relationship to be. Also, as I have said before, if this is PA behavior, the PA person wins if they can get the other to lose control and look bad.

This doesn't mean there is nothing she can do about the situation. But first, she needs to let go of the assumptions so that she can deal with it more directly. Once she does that, she could talk with her MIL but do it in a clear and assertive way. For instance: "The dress you've chosen is SO lovely! But I'm afraid it is so beautiful it will outshine me on my wedding day. Do you have another possible choice? I understand, though, if you really want to wear it."

This may not stop the MIL from wearing the dress, but it is more likely to establish a relationship in which the bride can discuss future problems with her directly. If the MIL does tend to be PA, knowing that her behavior will be discussed assertively and won't achieve the intended outcome of PA behavior (to make the other person lose control and look bad), tends to decrease it in the future.

Passive-aggressive Example 20 Parents' Criticism of Bride

Question: At my wedding my husband told a story about how he knew he liked me. He said I am a smart girl but I came to him to ask a work-related question. He also said I put my boot on the desk and asked if he liked them. I did ask but what he didn't tell everyone was that I was sitting at my own desk and they were modest ankle boots that I wore with bootleg slacks. I don't recall asking in a flirtatious manner but really as a concern because I wasn't sure I liked the boots as they were pointy and reminded me of an elf's boots. I didn't bother to say anything because I thought it was an entertaining story whether true or not. The next day my father suggested I was inappropriately promiscuous and demanded to know exactly how my relationship with my husband transpired! When I asked my husband to deal with him, my father said to my husband "between you and me I don't want it to go any further but she had problems coping with work." He also suggested he understood that my husband was helping me with work because I had problems indicating something inappropriate was happening. When I complained to my mother that dad was making up things my mother told me I argue with my father because I am just like him. Also, on the day of my wedding my father was teasing my mother with my wedding vows. I had given them the celebrant's program so they would know when to stand and give me away. On the day, they sat like stunned mullets and had to be prompted more than once to answer. I got angry at my mother for allowing my dad to use my program to tease her. She complained to my aunty that I gave her grief. It was one drama after another to do with really petty things. Almost all of it rumors, innuendo and lies from my father and my mother blaming me.

Response: I will assume that this wasn't a one-time experience with her parents. Instead, it is likely a pattern of behavior. However, she probably had the hope that her parents would behave differently at her wedding. The pattern appears to be a father who is critical, aggressive, and demanding and a mother who passive-aggressively backs him up. As a result, she is dealing with much more than passive-aggressive (PA) behavior.

The problem here is that her responses to her parent's behavior allows them to not only continue to behave this way but to blame her (in the typical PA fashion) whenever she complains. However, there are several things she can do to manage this situation better:

1) Extricate herself from this pattern.

Changing her way of responding to her parents is crucial because otherwise she is likely to play out a similar pattern with her husband (and children) in the future. There are a couple of clues that indicate this possibility: she is indirectly dealing with the conflict with her father through her mother and her husband. Indirectly confronting conflict is just another form of PA behavior. Therefore, by managing her father's behavior in a different way, she is also taking steps towards changing her own patterns learned while growing up in this family.

2) Stop complaining to her mother.

It doesn't appear that complaining does any good. In fact, it seems to have the opposite effect of heaping more blame on her. As I just indicated, it is also an indirect approach to dealing with conflict. If the problem is her father, she needs to leave her mother out of it.

3) Don't involve her husband in her problems with her family.

By having her husband confront her father she is just pulling her husband into the dysfunctional pattern. It provides her father with more opportunity to criticize and blame her. The problem with her family is her problem that she needs to manage herself.

4) Confront her father directly and assertively.

Being assertive means remaining calm. She must not confront him with anger because that will only backfire giving him ammunition to blame her for being unreasonable. Instead, assertive confrontation is calm with careful word choice. Her words need to be focused on what she has the ability to control and taking personal responsibility by using an "I" statement. For instance, when her father confronted her about being promiscuous and demanding to know more about her relationship, she could have responded (calmly), "I'm not going to discuss this with you." Most likely, he would have continued demanding: "I am your father! You WILL tell me!" However, she is an adult and can walk away from him using the technique of repeating the assertive statement, "I'm not going to discuss this with you."

5) Stop getting angry.

She needs to quit playing the blame game with her parents. For instance, she may be tempted to show her parents this response to validate her perception of their behavior, but they are likely to turn that against her as well. They are controlling her through her anger and then blaming her for the anger. She needs to recognize that she is not going to change them but she can change how she responds to them. She may not have control over them but she does have control over herself. When she quits expecting them to behave reasonably and learns to shrug off their behavior she will have greater control in her life.

Obviously, these parents are likely to continue to blame her even when she uses an assertive response. However, the difference here is that she maintains control over herself and doesn't engage in their dysfunctional pattern. The most important result is that her future is a direction of her (and her husband's) own making rather than continuing this family pattern of PA blaming.

Passive-aggressive Example 21 Is She Passive-aggressive or is She and Extrovert?

Question: My co-worker is always making statements that are said in jest, but always feel like a put down in some way. They feel like very passive-agressive comments. For example, I was in a meeting with a director and my co-worker and we were talking about collaboration and how effective it is. I said, "I love to collaborate" and my co-worker said, "YES!! You do! You REALLY LOVE to collaborate." I just smiled, but what does that even mean?

Also, I was talking about how I am shy when I meet people and I really have to work to break out of my shell. And she said laughing, "Are you kidding? I ALWAYS see you talking to random people all day long." I responded with, "I don't know who you see me talking to ALL day, but it's usually someone I am working on a project with. And yes, I do try to talk to people I don't know because I work to improve myself by getting out of my shell."

I often feel on the defense with her, like I always have to defend who I am as a person. It's really annoying and part of me wants to tell her that she needs to get some help to discover the underlying cause of her passive-aggressive behavior. But then I am letting her know it irritates me and that I am letting her get to me.

Response: What you describe could be passive-aggressive (PA) behavior or it could just be extroverted behavior. An introvert can often feel defensive with an extrovert because it seems as if they are being attacked by the comments. However, the extrovert may not mean them as attacks and they truly are simply joking statements. Therefore, it is not a good idea to directly suggest that she is PA because if it is not PA behavior you will look like the one who needs help.

The good news is that you can develop a response that can address the situation whether she is PA or whether she is an extrovert. So if she is making PA put-down jokes you can respond in a way that is likely to decrease the behavior because she is unable to irritate you. Keep in mind that the purpose of true PA behavior is to irritate you without having to take responsibility. By being indirect the PA person can deny if confronted with the behavior. Which is likely to happen in this case if your co-worker is being PA.

However, if she is not engaging in true PA behavior, then your responses will just seem like normal conversation but the behavior is unlikely to decrease. So, the responses you described are fairly good responses. Your first response of just smiling is good whether it is PA behavior or whether it is just meant as conversation. However, you might want to reduce the defensiveness in the second example you gave. For instance, "I guess if it seems that way to you, my efforts at being more social must be working!" This is a little more light-hearted, non-defensive response which works whether she is an extrovert or PA.

If what you have been doing has not reduced the behavior and given that she tends to exaggerate a great deal, I suspect it is likely she is an extrovert. However, I can't be certain without further information. I often see a lot of confusion, and sometimes conflict, between extroverts and introverts because they view the world in different ways. It is not that one way is right and one is wrong. They are just different. I learned this the hard way with my husband who is an extreme extrovert. At first I thought he didn't care if he embarrassed me but that never quite made sense because I knew he cared. Over time, I came to realize that we see the world differently.

Passive-aggressive Example 22

Is it Passive-aggressive or is it Aggressive?

Question: My angry adult daughter (who has to live at home right now) didn't acknowledge Mother's Day. I didn't say a word. When she didn't acknowledge Father's Day yesterday, I texted her asking if she was aware it was Father's Day and if this was a PA issue. Her response was, "Yes and it isn't passive."

Response: Several issues come to mind with this example. The first is what is the difference between PA communication and aggressive communication? The second is can PA communication ever be appropriate? And the third is how to respond to this type of communication.

1) The Difference Between PA and Aggressive

Although this daughter indicated by her response that she thought ignoring Father's Day was either aggressive or assertive communication (because she indicated it was not passive), I would disagree. The definition of PA communication is angry, indirect communication. In other words, if the receiver of the communication has to ask what are the intentions of the communicator, then it is likely to be PA. Passive communication is not communicating at all so the receiver doesn't even know there is a message. Aggressive communication is in your face: "I HATE you! I don't want to celebrate Father's Day!" Assertive communication is direct, but civil: "I think Father's Day is an arbitrary holiday contrived to sell cards and ties" or "I am angry with how you treat me and I don't want to celebrate Father's Day."

2) Can PA Communication Ever Be Appropriate?

I don't know this family's circumstances. However, I always tell my clients that any form of communication can be appropriate, but it depends on your goal. For instance, aggressive communication can be appropriate if you don't have the goal of an ongoing relationship and only want to vent your anger. But if you care about your relationship you may need to express your anger more assertively. PA communication can be appropriate when someone doesn't care about the relationship but also doesn't feel that any other expression of anger is safe (either because of the recipient's reaction or her own inability to contain it).

3) How Can This Parent Respond?

First, I would recommend to never confront suspected PA behavior in a text. I understand that sometimes that seems like the only available way to communicate. However, I think texting in this circumstance is a PA communication itself because it is not directly confronting a problem face-to-face. In addition, asking someone if their behavior is PA is also PA communication because it is a way of indirectly blaming or expressing anger. Since this is an "angry daughter" it would be much better to model appropriate assertive behavior for her: "I was hurt that you didn't want to celebrate Father's Day with us. Is there a problem? Let's talk about it." Such a response is more likely to lead to a discussion of the actual problem, and if it doesn't, at least the parent modeled an appropriate response to PA behavior.

Passive-aggressive Example 23 Confronting a Passive-aggressive Insult

Question: "You know that you shouldn't eat before bedtime, right?" said by brother-in-law (BIL) to overweight mother of nursing baby while she is eating a snack. Said with a giggle. They don't even know each other well and he is staying in their house for the first time.

Response: Maybe this is just a clueless man, i.e. the last man in the world who doesn't know that a man should never comment on a woman's weight directly or indirectly! However, let's say that he is aware which means that this is a passive-aggressive (PA) insult. He would probably disagree and say "But I was only trying to provide helpful information." Yet, any overweight woman knows that this is a comment on her weight. If his sister-in-law (SIL) was average weight he wouldn't have made such a statement. So the only reason to make this statement is to indicate that his SIL needs to watch her eating habits and lose weight.

This is a common PA tactic when a person doesn't have the guts to say what they are thinking because they KNOW it would be rude and the other person is likely to become angry. Instead, they guise it as advice so that if they are confronted, they can deny their true intentions. This BIL even added a giggle to it to give himself another out: "I was only kidding."

The question is how to respond to this behavior. In this case, I think a more direct approach would be appropriate:

SIL: "Are you INTENDING to insult me?"

BIL: "No...I was just trying to be helpful."

SIL: "Do you seriously believe that women find it helpful when you comment on their eating habits?"

This is likely to cause him to mumble something and back off. He is also not likely to make a similar mistake again. However, there are other ways to confront him if the SIL is not comfortable with such a direct approach:

SIL: "Why are you telling me this?" This statement puts him on the spot because then he has to refer to the weight as his true intention which he doesn't want to do. As I have addressed elsewhere PA people don't want to be direct as then they have to be responsible for what they say.

BIL: "..uh...eating before bedtime causes weight gain."

This allows the SIL to confront his true intention:

SIL: "So you are commenting on my weight and eating habits?" or "So you are telling me that I'm fat?"

Obviously, there are many approaches to this issue depending upon the personality of the individual and the kind of relationship. The primary goal, however, is to let the PA person know that they will be confronted when they use PA insults. As they are typically trying to avoid direct conflict this approach is likely to reduce the behavior. In this situation since they don't know each other very well, it informs him early in their relationship that she won't tolerate PA behavior.

Passive-aggressive Example 24 Living with Blaming and Guilting Mother (Part 1)

Question: My partner's mum is staying with us and she's quite PA and I'd love to know better ways of dealing with some of what she does...

A) She blamed my partner for not telling me her plans had changed (in the last thirty minutes) and that she did want me to include her for dinner after all. But she didn't tell him she now wanted to eat but only that she was leaving later. She didn't tell me (the person cooking) anything. We offered to split what we had but she made a fuss whilst making a sandwich and saying "I suppose you don't want to share!" Sporadically through the next hour she'd sigh and say to herself "it wouldn't have taken you both MUCH effort to pad out the meal" and "you've got to start passing messages."

B) Partner's mum is upset dishwasher wasn't run overnight. She complains to my partner loudly enough that I can hear: "I know she doesn't CARE about keeping the house tidy but how could anyone NOT run the dishwasher? Why on earth WOULDN'T you?"

Partner: "That's a little unfair when you make these general statements. I know she cares and she must have had a reason."

Mum: "Why on earth wouldn't you! It's just common sense!" (In fact I hadn't run it because she'd often complained about running it when it wasn't totally full and had even unpacked the top row to demonstrate that you could jam one more glass inside. This time the dishwasher had five or six spaces.)

Partner: "I would like you to think about maybe not making general statements. It upsets people."

Mum: "I'm not allowed to think anything! I've just got to shut up and keep my thoughts to myself. You want me gone. You make it totally clear you HATE having me here!"

Partner: "We like you here. I just want you to know people feel hurt if..."

Mum: "I'm not ALLOWED to say anything!!" Slams door, sulks in room. We leave her to it. Returns two hours later to scream at partner that he's a hateful (expletive)! Slams sitting room door. More sulking.

C) Partner's mum recites lists of what she does for us to her other children. She makes it sound as if we want her running after us and she's totally put upon. We'd rather tidy after ourselves but can't stop her doing this stuff:

Partner (working from home in personal office): "I don't like you coming in here every hour or so to see if I've got any cups. I'll take this cup once I've finished what I'm working on."

Mum: "I'll just take it."

Partner: "I don't want you to. It's distracting and I feel bad like you're slaving after me."

Mum: "I suppose you WANT the house to turn into a sty. You don't mind the house being DISGUSTING."

D) She has a lot of esteem wrapped up in having been an amazing mother and homemaker. If I choose to do a home-based task differently from how she would have, she will nitpick and point out the many flaws with doing it that way. She'll also say I did it that way because I "don't really CARE" and "that's a lazy way" to do that. Anything that's done her way is just "the way it SHOULD be done" and "why would anyone NOT do it that way!" Despite this she claims she doesn't get ANYTHING done her way although every room in the house is layed out how she wanted and most home things are done her way. When she returns from holidays she spends the next week pointing out things I've missed or supposedly done wrong: "I see it was too hot to mow the lawn!" (I'd mowed three days earlier). "I see no one could be BOTHERED to buy a new salt shaker! You guys!" Shakes her head. Salt shaker is still 3/4's full.

Response: As this is a very involved situation because it is a pattern of behavior that is quite hurtful and frustrating, I need to discuss this in several parts. In this post, I will point out some of the general issues to consider. Later, I will discuss some specific ways to address the different situations.

This mother is exhibiting classic PA behavior of the blaming and guilting type. As I've written before, it is important to understand the reward in the behavior to help determine an appropriate response. In other words, this couple needs to determine how the PA behavior is rewarded and stop rewarding the mother's behavior.

This concept of reward can be confusing as it does not seem that conflict could be rewarding. However, it can be in several ways. The first, and perhaps the most obvious, way this behavior might be rewarded is that the mother gets what she wants. This appears to be so when the writer describes how she needs to approach a simple task such as loading a dishwasher. Instead of just doing the dishes she considers how the mother might react. The fact that she is considering the mother's potential reaction indicates that the mother probably is rewarded for her behavior by getting her way. To address this type of reward the writer needs to determine how she would do things if she didn't consider the mother's possible reaction and then do it that way. Walking on eggshells is not going to prevent conflict. In fact, by always being fearful of the mother's potential reaction and giving into her, the writer is rewarding the PA behavior which is likely to increase it rather than decrease it.

Another way the mother may be rewarded is through the escalation of the conflict. Again, conflict may not seem to be rewarding to the emotionally healthy person. However, conflict can be a release of emotions as well as self-esteem building (in an artificial way). This mother can present herself as a martyr to other people and get positive attention in return which can allow her to feel better about herself. In addition, if there are negative emotions she is not confronting such as grief or loss in her life, the escalation of conflict can allow her to release those emotions. Certainly, this is not a healthy release of emotions as it displaces the emotions onto the other person but it still feels rewarding to the system. In other words, she feels better after the release and this couple feels worse. A classic example of displacement of emotions is that a man is yelled at by his boss, he comes home and yells at his wife, she yells at their son who then kicks the dog.

As I've mentioned in other posts, the PA person escalates the conflict in such a way that they can blame the other person. By doing so, they can deny responsibility and view themselves as the victim rather than the perpetrator. This type of approach allows them to feel justified in their behavior. By not engaging in a way that allows for the escalation, the couple forces the mother to have to deal with her emotions rather than displacing them.

This couple must feel they are being held hostage to this mother's behavior. She is sharing living expenses with them so from their perspective they do not have the power to enforce limits on her. Even if they were in a different position, they may desire to maintain a relationship with her. In any case, the first step is understanding her behavior. My article Why Are People Mean? Don't Take It Personally! may aid in this process. In particular, most people with mean behavior are motivated by their own personal issues. For instance, one clue in this situation is "She has a lot of esteem wrapped up in having been an amazing mother and homemaker." We don't know the entire situation for this woman. Has she always been like this? Has it gotten worse? If it has, what was the trigger? Does she feel as if she's been displaced? That she's no longer needed? Some women whose identities are focused on being a mother feel threatened by the "other woman" when their sons are in a relationship.

However, understanding her behavior does not justify it. Instead, it allows us to make some decisions regarding how to address it. For instance, if her behavior is based upon her own self-esteem issues, we would not consider it malicious. However, it is still hurtful, and even abusive. But since it is not malicious, it is possible that the relationship can be salvaged while responding to the PA behavior. This couple should consider that she needs them maybe even more than they need her. She not only needs them for financial reasons but also for her identity as a mother. She desires to feel needed and wanted. This is evidenced by some of her statements such as "You make it totally clear you HATE having me here!" If this is the case, it may also allow this couple to reward more desired behavior while they are trying not to reward the PA behavior. For instance, if she makes a genuinely helpful comment, they could make over it a bit more: "Oh, that is a great idea! It's wonderful having someone with your years of experience to guide us!" I understand at first this may be very difficult to do without gagging due to the tension that already exists in the relationship. However, it can be a useful strategy when combined with confronting her PA behavior.

Before this couple can address their communication with their mother, they need to address their own thinking. Although the son is trying to stand up to her and set limits, he seems to be concerned about confronting and upsetting his mother. This is understandable given her tendency to escalate conflict. However, making vague statements such as "I would like you to think about maybe not making general statements. It upsets people" does not set firm limits with her. I will discuss in later posts how to do this more explicitly. However, before he can be more firm, he needs to address his thinking that may be interfering. For instance, is he concerned about escalating the conflict? If so, he needs to recognize that she will escalate it no matter what because that is the tactic she is taking. By recognizing this he can decide on the message he wants to deliver and the limits he wants to set rather than confronting her vaguely due to the concern about how she may react.

This is just one possibility regarding how he is thinking when approaching the situation. To examine other possibilities, the couple needs to question themselves regarding the different options presented in the following posts and what might interfere with pursuing the option.

Passive-aggressive Example 25 Living with Blaming and Guilting Mother (Part 2)

I will examine and discuss the previous question in parts (for the full situation see Part 1).

Question: My partner's mum is staying with us and she's quite PA and I'd love to know better ways of dealing with some of what she does...

Partner's mum is upset dishwasher wasn't run overnight. She complains to my partner loudly enough that I can hear: "I know she doesn't CARE about keeping the house tidy but how could anyone NOT run the dishwasher? Why on earth WOULDN'T you?"

Partner: "That's a little unfair when you make these general statements. I know she cares and she must have had a reason."

Mum: "Why on earth wouldn't you! It's just common sense!" (In fact I hadn't run it because she'd often complained about running it when it wasn't totally full and had even unpacked the top row to demonstrate that you could jam one more glass inside. This time the dishwasher had five or six spaces.)

Partner: "I would like you to think about maybe not making general statements. It upsets people."

Mum: "I'm not allowed to think anything! I've just got to shut up and keep my thoughts to myself. You want me gone. You make it totally clear you HATE having me here!"

Partner: "We like you here. I just want you to know people feel hurt if..."

Mum: "I'm not ALLOWED to say anything!!" Slams door, sulks in room. We leave her to it. Returns two hours later to scream at partner that he's a hateful (expletive)! Slams sitting room door. More sulking.

Response: I'm starting with this example because it provides the opportunity to practice basic skills that can then be built upon. The first thing for this couple to keep in mind is that they do not need to provide reasons or excuses to justify their behavior. In fact, they do not want to even engage in this argument. The best technique for managing this is the "broken record." What this means is to have one or two assertive statements that are repeated over and over with only minor variations. It may be followed with some sort of limit such as "I'm not going to discuss this any further."

The key is developing a statement that places the responsibility back on the PA individual. As discussed in previous posts, PA behavior is about attacking or expressing anger in such a way that the individual can deny responsibility or the purpose of the attack. Therefore, it is important to address very specific behavior and to stay away from interpretations of behavior. For instance, "I feel hurt when you say that" is about a particular statement and the reaction to it whereas "You don't care if you hurt me" is interpreting the purpose of the statement.

This couple needs to develop a statement that they can say repeatedly in a variety of similar circumstances. For instance, "we have our own ways of doing things" or "I'm not going to listen to criticism." Let's try these out:

Mum: "I know she doesn't CARE about keeping the house tidy but how could anyone NOT run the dishwasher? Why on earth WOULDN'T you?"

Partner: "We have our own ways of doing things."

Mum: "Why on earth wouldn't you! It's just common sense!"

Partner: "We have our own ways of doing things."

Mum: "It's just common sense!"

Partner: "We have our own ways of doing things."

Mum: "Well, I guess I'm not allowed to have an opinion around here!"

Partner: "You can have an opinion but I'm not going to listen to criticism."

Mum: "I'm not ALLOWED to say anything!"

Partner: "All I said was that I'm NOT going to listen to criticism."

This won't stop her from slamming doors, sulking, and screaming which she is going to do no matter how this couple responds. However, it does put her on notice that they are not going to engage with her by giving excuses or trying to change their behavior to suit her. When she escalates, they can walk away saying "I'm not going to discuss this any further." Hopefully, over time she will learn that she is not going to get any satisfaction by engaging in this type of behavior and they may see a decrease in it. However, it is similar to a child throwing a temper tantrum. If the parent ignores the tantrum there may be an initial escalation but as the parent continues to ignore the tantrums a reduction in the length or frequency is likely to occur.

Another important aspect of this type of response is that they are focused on what they have control over. In particular, they have control over whether they want to engage with her. This differs from when her son says "I would like you to think about maybe not making general statements" with which he is trying to change her behavior but it only results in handing control over to her. This way he maintains control by saying "I'm not going to listen" or by walking away. The PA person wants to be the one in control and this is not likely to be satisfying for her. Therefore, the more this couple maintains control, the less she is rewarded for the PA behavior (see discussion in Part 1).

Passive-aggressive Example 26 Living with Blaming and Guilting Mother (Part 3)

I will examine and discuss the previous question in parts (for the full situation go to "Previous").

Question: My partner's mum is staying with us and she's quite PA and I'd love to know better ways of dealing with some of what she does...

Partner's mum recites lists of what she does for us to her other children. She makes it sound as if we want her running after us and she's totally put upon. We'd rather tidy after ourselves but can't stop her doing this stuff:

Partner (working from home in personal office): "I don't like you coming in here every hour or so to see if I've got any cups. I'll take this cup once I've finished what I'm working on."

Mum: "I'll just take it."

Partner: "I don't want you to. It's distracting and I feel bad like you're slaving after me."

Mum: "I suppose you WANT the house to turn into a sty. You don't mind the house being DISGUSTING."

Response: There are two issues to address in this situation: what she is saying to other family members and what the mother is doing. In regards to her talking to others this couple needs to recognize that they can't stop her from talking but they may be able to do some damage control. First, most likely, other family members know the way she is. Keeping that in mind this couple can develop some sort of statement they can say to others that will refute her version of the situation without being a direct confrontation. Remember, as I have said before, PA people usually will win direct confrontations because they are good at setting up the situation to be able to deny responsibility or an opposing perspective. In this situation the couple could use a bit of humor with a very subtle nonverbal indicating that they do not really think it is funny. Such as "You know Mum--you can't stop her from being a mother no matter how hard you try!" with a slight shake of the head and a very slight eye roll (the nonverbals not being in her line of sight). I know this is using passive-aggressive communication in response but sometimes you DO need to fight fire with fire. All types of communication are acceptable as long as they help you to achieve your goal and the consequences have been considered. In this case, it tends to diminish the strength of her statements.

To stop the mother from cleaning up after them, they may need to be more direct. This mother does not respond to an expression of feelings in the way most people would expect. In other words, telling her that it makes him feel bad doesn't have any impact on her behavior. Also, for this mother a statement such as "I don't like you coming in here..." is actually indirect. He needs to tell her more directly "I'm working. Don't come in" and use that as a broken record as we discussed in Part 2:

Mum: "Let me get your cup."

Partner: "I'm working. Don't come in."

Mum: "I'll just take it."

Partner: "No. I'm working. Don't come in."

Mum: "I suppose you WANT the house to turn into a sty. You don't mind the house being DISGUSTING."

Partner: Closes the door.

In the next part I will talk more about shaping her behavior which I briefly mentioned in Part 1.

Passive-aggressive Example 27 Living with Blaming and Guilting Mother (Part 4)

I will examine and discuss the previous question in parts (for the full situation go to "Previous").

Question: My partner's mum is staying with us and she's quite PA and I'd love to know better ways of dealing with some of what she does...

She has a lot of esteem wrapped up in having been an amazing mother and homemaker. If I choose to do a home-based task differently from how she would have, she will nitpick and point out the many flaws with doing it that way. She'll also say I did it that way because I "don't really CARE" and "that's a lazy way" to do that. Anything that's done her way is just "the way it SHOULD be done" and "why would anyone NOT do it that way!" Despite this she claims she doesn't get ANYTHING done her way although every room in the house is layed out how she wanted and most home things are done her way. When she returns from holidays she spends the next week pointing out things I've missed or supposedly done wrong: "I see it was too hot to mow the lawn!" (I'd mowed three days earlier). "I see no one could be BOTHERED to buy a new salt shaker! You guys!" Shakes her head. Salt shaker is still 3/4's full.

Response: This piece of information provides us with a clue as to how this couple may be able to change the situation. When we can understand why a person acts in the way they do, then we can manipulate the person to change. I'm using the word "manipulate" deliberately here because most people are reactive to a situation rather than proactive. Manipulation has often gotten a bad reputation because people think of it when it is used in a negative way. However, manipulation can also be used to change things in a positive way. For instance, when we use behavior modification of rewarding a child intermittently (i.e. not every time) for cleaning his/her room, we are manipulating that child to value cleaning the room. We can do the same thing with adults when we understand what underlies their behavior. In other words, when we know what motivates a person it allows us to use that motivator for rewarding desired behavior.

What we know about this mother is that her self-concept involves being a good mother and what that seems to mean to her is that she teaches her children how to behave in the "correct" way. However, she is no longer in that role because her children are grown up. Yet, she doesn't know how to show that she cares except by doing or telling others what to do. Obviously, this couple should not reward her by behaving in the way that she desires but they can teach her other ways to feel helpful and important rather than feeling like an old discarded shoe. I understand that it would be nice if you could just tell people directly that they should change their behavior, but that doesn't work with some people. It especially doesn't work with people who are in denial about their behavior. This mother probably doesn't believe she is being mean (because that would go against her self-concept of being a good mother) but genuinely believes she is trying to be helpful and others are just not appreciative of her.

However, as I said, this provides us with an important piece of information that can be used to change her behavior. I mentioned in the first post that when this mother does or says something that they like, then they can reward her because reward increases desired behavior. A reward for adults can simply be a positive statement or compliment: "Oh, that is a great idea! It's wonderful having someone with your years of experience to guide us!" Or, a reward can be asking for advice about something. Or, it can be saying something nice about her to others when she is present: "Mum is always trying to be helpful."

However, they need to be careful and combine this with the

assertive limit-setting when her behavior is inappropriate. Otherwise, they might just increase her overall "helpful" behavior which would include more criticism. Rather, they want to reward desirable behavior and punish undesirable behavior. Punishment in this case means not only not getting her way but also being confronted with the broken record, the closed door, the refusal to engage as discussed previously. Over time, she will learn at a subconscious level that she can "catch more flies with honey, than with vinegar."

I'm not saying they will be able to change her behavior but I've seen it happen more times than not when people take this type of approach with someone whose self-esteem is externally based. For more info, read: The Pillars of the Self-Concept: Self-Esteem and Self-Efficacy at ExcelAtLife.com.

Passive-aggressive Example 28 Child Holding Family Emotionally Hostage

Question: Daughter is asking for a guinea pig for Christmas and is stating if she doesn't get one she will stay in her room all day and make sure everyone else's day is bad, too. I am reluctant to get her one because I got her a hamster with all the bells and whistles for her birthday in April and she decided she no longer wanted to care for it and let it go outside 8 weeks later.

Response: This is a great example of a passive-aggressive (PA) in training. If the parent gives in to this emotional blackmail, the daughter learns that PA behavior is the way to get what she wants. This creates a disruptive and difficult relationship with her parent (who will be looking for an escape by the time the daughter is a teenager). However, the issue isn't so much about her relationship with her parent, the problem is that it teaches her daughter that PA behavior is how to handle all future relationships.

In addition, given that this behavior is related to the care of animals, the daughter is learning that pets are disposable depending upon her emotional whims. This parent needs to consider what are the lessons the daughter needs to be taught. Sure, it is easier to give into a child's behavior to make them temporarily behave. But it is at the cost of the child's future because what she learns now is how she will behave in the future. Does this parent want the daughter to grow up being PA in her relationships and treating everyone as if they exist to serve her and throwing them away when they no longer suit her? Children don't magically change when they become adults. Instead, they become what they are taught.

This parent needs to stand her ground and teach her daughter that this is not acceptable behavior. The parent shouldn't argue, explain, or otherwise engage with the daughter except to say, "No, you are not ready to have a pet." Repeat as necessary. If the daughter wants to stay in her room all day--fine! Let her stay in her room. And if she comes out of the room trying to make everyone miserable, put her back in the room. She can't make everyone miserable unless they allow her. The rest of the family should focus on enjoying their Christmas without her and including her only when she chooses to behave. Does this make for a pleasant Christmas? Perhaps not. But isn't the lesson for her future more important than any one day in the present? The responsibility of parents is to teach children appropriate behavior for their future, not to make sure the child is always happy in the present (even if it is Christmas).

Under no condition should this daughter have another pet until she learns how to treat people better and understands the value of other living creatures. Holding people emotionally hostage is not appropriate. And throwing animals outside to die is not appropriate, either. However, the only way to teach her these lessons is through setting limits and applying consequences to her behavior (explaining, cajoling, arguing doesn't work). The consequence of not caring for a pet is that she is not ready to have another one. The consequence for trying to make everyone miserable to get what she wants is that she can be miserable by herself in her room.

Passive-aggressive Example 29 Got His Way at a Cost

Question: I am the youngest of five brothers. Throughout my life I had crying fits to get what I wanted: bicycles, minibikes, motorcycles, cars. Even though I got what I wanted, I was ridiculed at family holiday gatherings: "He always gets what he wants!" My parents would give in to me but then I paid for it by them being angry with me about it. I thought to myself, "Why did Mom and Dad give in to me in the first place" and then make me pay emotionally?

Response: This example is sort of the other side of the coin from the previous example of "Child Holding Family Emotionnally Hostage" as this one shows the view of the child. Frequently, when children get their way in a passive-aggressive family it is at a cost. In this way, the parents can disavow themselves of any responsibility and place it on the children. In other words, they can believe they are being good parents while the child is being a brat: "He always gets what he wants!" What they don't realize is that if a child always gets his (or her) way, it is because the parents aren't effective parents. The job of a parent is to teach a child how to behave in an adult world.

The adult world won't give this young man everything he wants just because he has a winning smile or throws a fit. In fact, more likely, this man is now handicapped in the adult world. He may not know how to interact in an appropriate way to achieve his goals, unless, hopefully, he has developed awareness of the errors in his childhood lessons and made deliberate efforts to change. Parents who give in to children teach them to be obnoxious adults who have trouble in relationships and working with others.

When my son was young, I would say "no" to him just for practice. My practice and his. Parents don't want to say "no" because it doesn't feel good. They want their children to be happy and have what they want. But to be a good parent we must set limits. Keeping that in mind, I practiced saying "no" with the little things that didn't matter so that I would be able to say "no" with the big things. That also gave my son the practice of learning how to accept "no." In fact, when he was about 17, he said to me, "Mom, I'm glad you didn't spoil me. My friends who got everything they wanted are hard to get along with."

The lesson for today is set limits and say "no" to your children. Even though a tantrum-throwing child can be quite unpleasant, becoming a tantrum-throwing adult is even worse.

Passive-aggressive Example 30 "I will take care of it, just as I ALWAYS do!"

Question: When I don't respond to my wife's request as quickly as she believes I should, she heaves a sigh and says "I will take care of it, just as I ALWAYS do!" I find this very irritating as I intended to do what she wanted but instead I am criticized for not responding on her time schedule. How do I handle this without getting in a big argument?

Response: This deceptively simple statement is difficult to respond to because it is a passive-aggressive trap. Typically, the purpose is for the perpetrator to be able to expound on her martyrdom. If you disagree in any way, it gives her the opportunity to express how no one appreciates her and everything she does. If you ignore it, it allows her to continue to feel like a martyr and to complain about how she takes care of everything. If you try to confront her about her behavior, she bursts into tears about how she's being criticized just for being helpful. The "always" in her statement is particularly a trap because it opens the door for you to argue that she is being unduly harsh in her criticism. Which, more than likely, allows her to ignore you and bring it back to her martyrdom: "It just seems that I'm having to do everything!" It is a perfect trap...almost.

As I've indicated elsewhere, the primary thing you want to do with PA behavior is to not reward the other person by responding in a way to achieve their goals. The less reward for a person's behavior, the less likely they will continue. In this instance, any response as described above that allows her to feel like a martyr will be rewarding to her. So, you need to assess her likely reaction to your response and find one that is not rewarding.

One possibility, for example, is to focus on your feelings. This makes it more difficult for her to focus on her feelings of martyrdom.

You (very calmly): I feel hurt that you think I wasn't going to do this.

Her (some sort of denial): That's not what I meant.

You: I want to help you and it hurts when you think I won't.

Her: Well, I asked you an hour ago and its not done.

You (using the broken record technique of repeating how you feel): I intended to help and I feel hurt that you think I wasn't going to.

Her: But I needed it done right away!

You: I didn't know that and I feel hurt when you believe that I won't help you.

If you notice with this scenario, she is getting defensive which means she is not able to maintain her martyr role. As a result, this type of confrontation can be more effective in reducing this statement in the future.

Passive-aggressive Example 31 Insulted by Thank You Notes as a Gift

Question: When I graduated from college my aunt gave me a box of thank you cards along with a generous amount of cash. I feel the thank you notes were a passive-aggressive insult implying that I don't have proper manners. How do I respond to this?

Response: This is a good example to show why it is important not to respond to all passive-aggressive behavior. At times, even though you might believe the behavior is PA, it might not be. Also, sometimes the best response is the same response whether it is PA or not.

Let's look at this situation a little more in depth. First, are all gifts of thank you cards insults or passive-aggressive messages? No, it depends upon the circumstances. For example, I was at a 50th Jubilee for a friend who is a member of a convent and I notice that she received many gifts of thank you cards. I don't think the other nuns were being PA! I think they found some attractive note cards they thought she would be able to use for gifts and other acknowledgments of thanks. So, it is possible that if a person does send out thank you cards routinely, other people may think it is a good gift. It's possible her aunt thought they would be useful. For instance, her aunt may have had her future job search in mind.

However, let's say that the aunt is being PA because previously her niece did not acknowledge gifts. This could be an example of the aunt not being able to directly communicate rather than deliberately being insulting. Instead, the aunt, intending to be helpful and teach her niece to show appreciation of gifts from others, may have communicated this indirectly by giving the thank you notes rather than confronting her niece. In that case, she was not trying to insult her niece but trying to teach important manners that she needs in life.

So, what should this person do? The nice thing about this type of situation is that the answer is the same no matter what the aunt had in mind: thank her for the cards! If she truly thought she was being helpful, such a response is the most appropriate. If she was being PA, then it is best to not acknowledge the PA behavior but to listen to the message. In fact, if the niece has truly been remiss in writing thank you notes, she could even address that: "Thank you for the note cards. They will help remind me to acknowledge people such as yourself who have been so generous." If the aunt's gift was PA, then this response also models direct communication.

Passive-aggressive Example 32 Adult Son Deliberately Upsetting Mother

Question: I had my son and my lovely daughter-in-law over for dinner. My son invaded the kitchen space and started to turn the burners down when I turned them up. The potatoes burned and I put on a new batch which only took a few moments to do. He continued switching the burners on and off. He said I was trying to impress which I was not. His eyes were dark and angry. I was so upset I was shaking hours later. This is not the first time I felt like this. He comes back and says he is sorry afterward but it takes me a long time to recover from his behavior.

Response: Often when people submit questions to me, they are describing their side of the story when there is usually more that is occurring. In such situations, I need to read between the lines because sometimes when inexplicable PA behavior occurs (the son's in this situation) it indicates that PA behavior may be occurring on both sides. However, the mother is unaware of her own PA behavior. What she needs to think about is what are the messages her behavior is giving to her son?

Keep in mind that I am making assumptions based upon very little information and could be completely wrong about this situation. However, this is a training exercise to help people recognize and handle PA behavior so whether my conclusions apply to this particular situation doesn't matter as much as how to handle situations that do meet my assumptions.

This mother probably responded to his behavior by telling him to stop and when he didn't, saying "See, now the potatoes are burned!" Including the information that it "only took a few moments" to put on a new batch indicates they most likely had words about her needing to redo the potatoes. "Mom, they're fine. You're just trying to impress." This speculation and the fact that he does this sort of thing and then apologizes later indicates that most likely this is a perfectionistic mother and a son who is unable to communicate his feelings. Therefore, this is probably a passive-aggressive (PA) duo.

The son seems to be angry with his mother which is often the purpose of PA behavior: an indirect way of expressing anger. If his mother confronts him about his anger, his PA response is likely to be, "I'm just messing with you. You're too uptight." The question is "Why is he angry with his mother?" From what she is describing it seems this is a long-term behavior pattern. He could be angry with her for something specific or it could be the nature of their relationship. Or, it could be a learned behavior that allows him to transfer his frustration about other things onto his mother.

As I indicated, the mother's behavior is most likely PA as well. The perfectionistic martyr ("I'll just put on a new batch of potatoes") gives the indirect message of "You are the cause of my suffering." She then has an anxiety attack to emphasize her point. This is an indirect (PA) consequence to her son. Of course, he is angry with her! Who wants to be told they are the cause of their mother's suffering? One of the most difficult mothers to deal with is the perfectionistic mother because she comes across as only having the child's best interest in mind. That is difficult to confront directly and so children develop other ways to show anger. It is important for her to recognize that her PA style could be the root of his anger. Once she understands that, then she has options to truly change this situation.

How can she stop this pattern with her son? She doesn't seem to provide direct consequences. If she did, he wouldn't be in her kitchen. First, when he does something like this, she should stop and let him suffer the consequences. A lot of times people believe that they can't set consequences for other adults because they don't have control. "I can't make him stop." But what many adults don't seem to realize is that even though they don't have control over the other's behavior, they do have control over their own. For example, she could quit cooking and say, "You can finish dinner. Or, if you want me to do the cooking, then you need to leave the kitchen." This is direct communication with a consequence attached. Or, if the potatoes are burned, serve them burned. But without a martyr statement ("He caused me to burn the potatoes").

Instead, she should take responsibility for her anxiety. He doesn't cause her to be upset and anxious, she allows him to do so because she doesn't give herself the option of setting limits and consequences. She should quit her PA communication of him causing her to be upset and instead learn methods to control her anxiety.

Obviously, there are changes the son could make as well, but he is not the one asking what to do.

Passive-aggressive Example 33 Handling a Backhanded Compliment

Question: How do you respond to the following statement? "Wow, for someone really well read, you watch the stupidest TV shows!"

Response: I suppose the temptation is to respond with, "Wow, for someone supposedly intelligent, you say the stupidest things!" However, let's assume that we don't want to stoop to the same level, but instead, handle this type of statement with tact while confronting the insult.

This is an example of a backhanded compliment which is a passive-aggressive way of insulting someone and can take many forms. Often, the insult is fairly well disguised but the recipient can distinguish the subtle nuance and feel the insult. However, in such a situation, it is very difficult to confront because on the surface it appears to be a compliment. As a result, the perpetrator can blame the victim if confronted, "Wow! Are you sensitive! I didn't mean it that way at all!"

In this case, however, the insult is fairly clear. I categorize it as a backhanded compliment because it starts out as a compliment and then slaps the victim in the face with an insult. Therefore, it can be confronted more directly: "I feel hurt when you judge me like that" or "Is there a reason you feel the need to criticize my TV viewing?" or "I understand you have a difference of opinion about TV shows, but is it necessary to say it in such a hurtful way?"

These statements confront the intention of the statement and point out how it is inappropriate. The other individual can still get defensive and deny intention such as "I was only kidding! You are so sensitive!" In which case, using the broken record technique of repeating what you just said (or a variation of it) with a request of

"I'd appreciate if you don't do that again" until the person quits being defensive and agrees with your request can be effective.

Passive-aggressive Example 34 Trap of Demanding Private Thoughts

Question: I'm working on my issues with jealousy. I try not to share my jealous thoughts and feelings with my girlfriend, but what do I say when she asks "What's wrong?" If I answer "I'm trying to work through some things" she demands to know what it is about and then we end up in an argument about the jealousy. What should I do?

Response: This is a good example of the need for privacy in a relationship. Some people have the romantic notion that all thoughts should be shared by a couple. And if thoughts are not shared, that person feels rejected: "If you can't share with me, that means you can't trust me!"

However, some thoughts shouldn't be shared. As human beings we have all sorts of thoughts. Part of living together in harmonious relationships is to sort through our thoughts and share what is appropriate. This is true of creating a harmonious society as well (although you wouldn't know it by what is broadcast by media today).

In this situation, he understands that he has a problem--a problem that has caused discord in his relationship when he shared it. He recognizes it is his problem to be solved and can't be solved as a couple. However, jealous feelings don't stop just because he recognizes they are inaccurate or says "Stop!" As readers of this website know, changing emotions requires repeated attention over a period of time to the thoughts that create the emotions. He is trying to do this. However, he still feels the emotion and may be quiet or withdrawn when trying to work through it.

His girlfriend knows he has a problem. She knows he is trying to work on it. When she demands that he tell her what is wrong after he has said he is working through his thoughts, she is setting him up to fail. Hopefully, this is unintentional and due to her need for reassurance and security. In which case, education can be helpful. Explaining to her how cognitive therapy works and that he is supposed to work through irrational thoughts privately because they have nothing to do with her may be enough to help her stop demanding.

If she continues to demand, then this could be a passive-aggressive (PA) trap. As I've written before, PA behavior is often for the purpose of escalating the situation in such a way as to place the blame on the other person. When this occurs it may be necessary to confront that behavior. However, with PA behavior, it is best not to confront too directly. For instance, don't say, "You are trying to start an argument." If you do, it provides the PA person with the perfect opportunity to turn the blame back on you.

Instead, perhaps ask why the person feels a need to know, "You know I'm working through some things that have nothing to do with you. And you know that if I share them it will cause an argument. Is there a reason you feel I need to share?" A rational person would likely back down at this point. However, if the girlfriend has her own unresolved issues, she could still persist, "Well, I want to know what you are thinking because it lets me know whether you still have a problem." The trap in this response is that it is like telling an alcoholic, "If you ever think about drinking, you can't be trusted." The fact that a person is addressing a problem is the important issue. Also, given that no one is perfect, the fact that a person recognizes a problem and thinks about it and tries to change the behavior associated with it, is the best sign of movement towards health.

If the girlfriend persists no matter what and escalates the argument, it is possibly an attempt to break up without having to be responsible for ending the relationship. Again, this can be confronted directly but by placing the responsibility on her: "I've told you the problem. I'm addressing it. But you continue to undermine my efforts by insisting that I share my thoughts. If you continue, I can only believe that you are wanting to escalate the conflict. If so, then you also have a problem to address or it means you want to leave. Let's discuss this directly rather than focusing on me expressing thoughts and feelings that I know are irrational."

Passive-aggressive Example 35 The Passive-Aggressive "Nice" Mother

Question: I'm an adult child living at home. My mother makes me so angry but she is always so nice about it. She'll tell me, "Honey, we're trying to treat you like an adult, but you're not thinking this through and making good decisions." Anything I try to do she finds fault with but she does it in a nice way, "Are you sure that is what you want to do?" I don't choose the right career. I can't eat right. I can't spend my time in the right way. Why can't I just make mistakes and learn from them? It's my life! If I get angry, she's just clueless and claims, "I'm just trying to help you become independent."

Response: This is one of the more difficult passive-aggressive (PA) scenarios because the mother probably isn't even aware of how she comes across and most likely has good intentions of "helping" her daughter. Often this occurs because the parent feels she has to raise her child "right" and doesn't want the child to make mistakes because that would reflect poorly upon her as a mother. The problem, however, is that it often leads to the child questioning herself, doubting herself, and unable to make decisions.

At least this person is getting angry about it which actually is a good sign. It means she recognizes that her mother is wrong and focusing on that rather than blaming herself and second-guessing herself. However, she is getting stuck on confronting her mother because her mother doesn't understand the effect of what she is doing. If the daughter tries to explain the effect her comments have, she can't see it. She truly believes that she is only trying to help. When her daughter becomes frustrated with trying to get her to understand and reacts angrily, it confirms in the mother's mind that the daughter has a problem.

In this situation, it is best for the daughter to have a single statement that she uses over and over whenever her mother tries to advise her such as: "Mom, I'm an adult and I'll make my own decisions."

Let's see how this might look. The daughter should remain calm throughout this interaction, otherwise the mother "wins" by showing that the daughter is unreasonable:

M: Don't you think you should get up earlier to look for a job?

D: Mom, I'm an adult and I'll make my own decisions.

M: But it just seems that you're more likely to get an interview...

D: I'm an adult and I'll make my own decisions.

M

: I'm just trying to help.

D: I know your trying to help, but I'll make my own decisions.

M: But I don't think you're making good decisions.

D: Then I'll handle that as an adult by making my own decisions.

M: But...

At this point the daughter should cut her off firmly but calmly: I'm not going to discuss this anymore. I will make my own decisions.

This may not stop the mother's behavior but it gives the daughter a way to respond. Such a response is an adult response which can help the daughter build her confidence. Otherwise the daughter becomes trapped in the childish response of frustration and anger which only proves to her mother that she can't handle her life.

Passive-aggressive Example 36 Another Passive-Aggressive Mother and Planning a Wedding

Question: I am having a very hard time planning my wedding because my mom and I want very different things. I believe in simplicity. Having a small intimate wedding (and a healthy marriage) is important to me, not a huge, traditional wedding. She wants to make decisions for me and demonstrates extreme passive-aggressiveness when I tell her my beliefs and what I want. She nicely says I can do whatever I want but then doesn't get excited about the things I decide on. It's hard because I want her to be excited but I also want to have the wedding I want. Yesterday we went dress shopping and before I could even say "yes" or "no" to the dress, she did. I ended up buying a dress that she liked. She told me the one I liked wasn't as slimming and the dress she liked made me look beautiful. She also ran into another bride in the store who was having a traditional wedding at a well known expensive venue in the area where she had wanted my wedding but I said "no" to because of the cost, stuffy atmosphere etc. When the girl asked where I was having it, my mom looked embarrassed to tell her my venue was at a bowling alley. It hurts. When I confront my mom she says I'm too sensitive and that I should just do everything on my own if I don't want her help. I want to note my mother is a beyond amazing person--would do anything for me. It's just that she is a very passive-aggressive person and plays dumb when confronted. Her image and appearance is very important to her and always has been. I feel like she thinks my decisions reflect on her image.

Response: It's interesting how often conflicts between mothers and daughters come about because of weddings. I think this is for a couple of reasons. One is the daughter is now an adult and making decisions for herself so the parent doesn't have as much control. Which causes the problem regarding the second issue. That is, conflict usually occurs when people have two different needs. In this case, the mother and daughter have different images and desires for the wedding.

Handling this situation is probably more about the bride dealing with her thinking about the situation and recognizing how that allows her passive-aggressive (PA) mother to control her. Important information in this scenario is that she indicates her mother is "amazing" but concerned about what other people think. This tells us that her mother is probably a social perfectionist in that she seeks approval from others by trying to do things "perfectly" or "right." She also expects her family to conform to her version of impression management. However, she also has the need to be the "perfect" mother so she tells her daughter she can do what she wants although she really would like her daughter to conform to what she believes is socially acceptable. When her daughter doesn't, she feels disappointed but is unable to voice this because that would not be her concept of the "perfect" mother. Therein lies the source of the PA behavior.

I have described before the purpose of PA behavior is to express anger without having to take responsibility for the anger. In this case, the mother feels her frustration/disappointment (anger) is unacceptable according to her standards for mothering so her feelings come out in a PA manner. She seems to be in denial of this behavior because such behavior would also be against her standards of mothering. However, the PA behavior allows her to try to control her daughter without having to recognize that she is a controlling parent (which wouldn't fit with her self-concept of "mother")

So, what can the daughter do? She's already tried confronting the behavior which hasn't worked. And probably won't work because her mother would have to change her entire self-concept. As a result, her mother deflects the daughter's confrontation with "You're too sensitive."

This is a situation that because the daughter is happy with her mother in other ways, she needs to change her own thinking rather than expecting her mother to change her behavior. First, she needs to ignore all PA messages. If her mother does not communicate directly, the daughter needs to let those messages just go over her head as if they didn't exist. Don't dwell on them--they are not a true message. Instead, listen to the directly communicated messages such as her mother stating she can do whatever she wants.

Second, the daughter needs to modify her expectations and recognize that she can't have it all. She can't have the wedding she wants without disappointing her mother and still have her mother excited about her choices. The mother had an image of the perfect wedding and she is grieving the loss of that image. Right or wrong, she can't easily let go of that image, and therefore, cannot be as excited about what the daughter wants. The daughter needs to let go of her expectation. Else, she is doing the same thing her mother is: having an expectation and being hurt when that expectation isn't met. I wonder if her anger is being communicated in a passive-aggressive way as well?

Parents can't always be what we want them to be. Children can't always be what we want them to be. The more she can accept her mother the way she is, the more she can enjoy the good parts of the relationship, and ignore the bad. Because, really, it doesn't sound like it is a "horrible" relationship.

Once the daughter has come to an acceptance of her mother's short-comings, she can then communicate directly about the wedding: "Mom, I know you are disappointed not to have the wedding you dreamed for me, but I want you to know that I think you are the greatest for being able to deal with your disappointment and let me have the wedding I dream of." Instead of conflict, the mother gets recognition for being a good mother (and might even be able to let go of the loss and provide the daughter with more acceptance, too).

Passive-aggressive Example 37 Husband and Wife Mutual Sulking

Question: I have been searching for the causes of frustration I have been going through with my husband for a while now, and I actually thought I was the passive aggressive one in the marriage because of all the sulking and mutual silent treatments. However it turns out I am only reflecting what is being imposed on me. For example, he does not do things I ask him to do. I am not fond of asking for people to do stuff for me. When I do, it usually is truly necessary that they do it. If I tell him to pick up the table after a meal I cooked and put on the table, he says "I would only do it if you don't tell me to do it." Next time I would not tell him what to do, expecting him to remember, and he just lets the table with dirty dishes sit there for hours and hours. He definitely knows I am expecting him to remove them so he resists me even when I don't say anything. When I become angry and try to tell him jokingly he starts the sulking/anger/resistance telling me I am once again trying to control him. So next time I just silently remove the dishes from the table and I sulk instead. When I sulk it causes him to sulk and we go days resenting each other. I don't understand it: if I don't ask him when I want him to do something, how will he ever know I want them done?

Response: Several problems are occurring in this scenario because both people are being passive-aggressive (PA). He clearly is putting her in a PA trap and she is falling into it and responding in a PA way herself. However, he is a master at it and will win every time so she needs to stop playing the game.

The biggest problem for their marriage is the sulking and silent treatment for days which can seriously poison a marriage. This is something the wife can do something about since she is a participant. She can't change his behavior directly but by her being more assertive and direct his behavior might change in response.

Therefore, she needs to stop her PA responses because all this does is escalate into a battle of who can out-PA the other. Let's start with "I become angry and try to tell him jokingly" because that is a clear PA behavior because it is an indirect expression of anger which is not lost on him. He knows at that point he has won the battle and his reward is to sulk while placing the blame on her. Instead of joking she needs to be direct. In fact, why become angry? Think of it like dealing with a child. With a child you don't become angry, you tell them what is acceptable and what are the consequences.

In this case, being direct would be saying something like, "I feel hurt when I ask for assistance and you ignore my request." Will he still get angry and sulk? Probably. But at least she is not participating in the PA contest.

However, let's imagine that instead of sulking right away, he responds, "You are trying to control me again."

She could say (with sincerity--not an angry tone), "I am asking for help--is there a better way for me to do that?"

He might say, "I will only do it if you don't tell me to do it."

At that point she could respond with (again, with sincerity), "I don't know how to make a request without asking you. Maybe it is the way I am asking? Is there another way to let you know when I need help?" This places the responsibility back on him instead of her remaining in his trap of "don't tell me, but if you don't ask me I won't do it."

If he continues to say in one form or another, "Don't ask" then she may have to engage in consequences. For instance, once when my family wasn't helping with the dishes without a lot of friction, I went on strike. I didn't say a word about it. I just stopped doing the dishes. I didn't do it angrily and didn't change my behavior in any other way--I simply told myself I wasn't going to do it. It took about two weeks and every dish in the house was dirty and piled up on the counters but one day I came home and the kitchen was clean. To this day I don't know who did them because I never commented on it. But I never had a problem after that.

Second, she needs to stop the sulking. This becomes easier if she assertively states how she feels. For instance, instead of "silently" removing the dishes she could do the dishes but make an assertive statement such as "I feel it is unfair when I do the cooking and you won't help me with clean up." Remember, assertive is direct, polite, to the point, and without an angry tone. Make the statement and then drop it. Don't continue to dwell on the situation. If he sulks, she should ignore the sulking and act normal. In this way, he can't win by getting her to escalate into a sulking match and then blaming her. If she doesn't participate, he's having to play by himself. Which isn't as much fun.

Passive-aggressive Example 38 Controlling by Refusing to Discuss Problems

Question: Any time I want to calmly discuss a situation that is bothering me in our relationship, my husband's reply is always "I don't want to fight about this!" Although I tell him that I'm not trying to fight, I just want to talk about it, he never has the discussion with me and the problems are always left unresolved.

Response: The husband's statement "I don't want to fight about this!" is a controlling trap because it allows the wife only two choices: drop the subject or continue to pursue. He actually is saying "I don't want to talk about this" so if she discontinues the conversation his controlling behavior is rewarded by getting what he wants. However, if she continues to pursue, he can shift all the blame on her by accusing her of "fighting." She has tried to explain that she is only wanting to talk but since the real meaning of his statement is "I don't want to talk about this" any conversation is viewed from his perspective as fighting. A perfect trap.

So, how can she get out of this trap? The best way is to avoid the trap completely. And the way to do that is to not have discussions about situations that are bothering her in the relationship. "What?!!" you might say. "That doesn't resolve her problem!" But it can--I will explain more thoroughly.

One clue as to what is occurring in this relationship is that she wants to "discuss a situation." This is a common practice for women who want to express their feelings and come to an understanding or resolution of a problem. Sounds reasonable, doesn't it? However, many women live with men who don't operate in the same way-- they don't want to discuss "feelings" and "relationship problems."

Seems to be an impasse. How can anything get resolved if one person wants to talk about it and the other person doesn't?

A solution to any problem is best addressed by the person who recognizes the problem and wants to change it. Therefore, in this situation the wife needs to make a change to accommodate her husband's style of communication. Specifically, the communication style for many men is often very direct, clear, and concise. If they don't like something, they say "I don't like that." If you do something that bothers them, they say "Stop that." Whereas women want to discuss their feelings and fully explain the problem so that the other person understands and no one gets their feelings hurt. This style might work great with other women but can present a problem in some relationships.

I came to understand these different communication styles when my son was a young teen. My tendency was to explain my reasoning for decisions so that he would understand. However, this approach just led to escalation of conflict. Until one day he said, "Mom, why can't you just say 'no'?" I thought, "Wow, that would be simpler!" As a result, I found that being more direct with him was much more effective.

Given these different communication styles, my suggestion to stop having "discussions" about a problem may make more sense. Instead of discussing a problem, she should just tell him directly what the problem is and what she wants him to do. For instance, instead of having a discussion about him not helping around the house, she needs to specifically tell him "I need you to do the dishes right after dinner." Or, if he is not affectionate enough, say "Give me a hug." If he does something that is hurtful, say "I feel hurt when you do that--don't do that again." I know these direct statements can be uncomfortable for many women, but being direct can solve many problems in relationships. And in this particular relationship, it avoids the controlling trap.

One other thing--many women react to this suggestion by saying "But then he'll say I'm nagging him." However, most men don't see these direct statements or requests as nagging. What they consider nagging is when criticizing, blaming, or labeling occurs: "I've asked you three times!" or "You just don't care" or "You never..." or "You are lazy."

Passive-aggressive Example 39 Confronting Step-son About Not Visiting

Question: I believe that my 41-year old step-son is being passive aggressive in refusing to visit us, alone or with his wife and two children. He knows that his mother had an affair (to whom she is now married) then divorced his father. I met his father a few years later, eventually moved in with him and his then 25-year old son, and we married two years later. His son deeply resented this as he thought he and his girl-friend would live with his father until he eventually inherited the property. He had resented other females with whom his father had had relationships after his divorce so it's not that he just didn't like me, he just didn't want his father to re-marry. My step-son doesn't openly refuse to visit us but gives inane excuses why he can't (such as my car is broken, I'm too busy, etc.) that insult our intelligence. My husband won't challenge him as he's his only child because my husband's daughter died tragically, aged 11, many years ago. He has visited us three times in the last 4 years, the first time coming to our new house out of curiosity but he refused to come to the house on the two subsequent visits and insisted we meet for lunch at a local restaurant at our expense. My step-son and his family did come to my husband's 70th birthday party 6 months ago but only, I feel, as he knew the rest of the family would be here and he didn't want to look bad in front of them by not attending. My step-son doesn't invite me or his father to visit them. If my husband asks when he can visit, his son tells him he's welcome any time and won't set a date but he lives 90 miles away so we can hardly call to see them. This behavior has become worse over the last 10 years but when asked what is the problem my step-son expresses surprise and says there's nothing wrong with them, the problem must lie with us. He and his wife often see her family and his mother and her new husband. If he were my son I would challenge him openly and ask for an explanation but my husband is reluctant to do this for fear of making the situation worse. I can no longer take the inane excuses for not visiting so it's inevitable that I will challenge my step-son on this soon. My husband loves children but, sadly, doesn't see his grand-children very often. I'm not allowed to consider them to be my grand-children, this is made very clear by my step-son and his wife referring to me by my first name when they mention me to the children in my presence. It's designed to be hurtful and it is hurtful but nothing we do changes the situation leading me to think that it is passive-aggressive behavior on my step-son's part.

Response: The first issue here is whether the step-son's behavior is passive-aggressive (PA) or not. The second issue is what the step-mother can do about it.

To answer the first question, let's look at the definition of PA behavior: the passive expression of anger (aggression) designed to not take responsibility for the anger by making it appear to be the recipient's problem. Examining this situation in light of this definition makes it clear that the step-son is engaging in PA behavior especially when he denies there is a problem (when clearly he and is family are not visiting) and shifts the blame to them.

However, knowing this and accusing him is not going to do any good and is likely to make things worse as the father fears. The step-mother wants to confront in an effort to protect her husband but she is likely to create additional problems. Any confrontation should come from the father and he is unwilling to do that (and a direct confrontation is not a good idea anyway when dealing with a PA person).

So, what can she do? First, this is her husband's problem, not hers. By accepting it as his problem she can resist the urge to try to correct it by confronting her step-son. No matter how much we care about someone, we can't effectively fix their problems without their consent. To try to do so is interfering and can create a host of other problems including, in this case, conflict or negative emotions between her and her husband. By accepting that it is her husband's problem she can also refrain from complaining to her husband about the step-son. Why allow this to be a negative interaction between the two of them? That allows the step-son to win because he is creating a problem for them without having to be responsible. Instead, she can console her husband when he is hurting and be a support for him: "I know it's difficult not being able to see your son and grandchildren."

Once she is able to let go of the problem, perhaps other solutions will appear. For instance, one possibility that I see is taking the step-son up on his offer to see them anytime. Even though it may be difficult, it is not impossible. The parents could start contacting the son on a regular basis (every couple weeks) and say "We're planning on stopping by this weekend. When is a good time for you?" Sure, they may be told "We're busy this weekend" but if they persist even after repeated rejections, then it becomes more clear where the problem lies. If that occurs, the father could ask "We've been trying to make arrangements to see you for the last several months. Is there a problem?" At that point it is more difficult for the son to shift the blame to them as they have been making an effort. It's also possible that maybe that won't even be necessary because the son might agree to the visits.

One last thing. The step-mother says she's not allowed to be a grandmother to these children. However, a grandmother is not a name--it is a relationship. For instance, my step-granddaughter was told by her grandmother that I was not her "real" grandmother. When she told me this, I asked "Do you think I love you?" She answered, "Yes." I hugged her and said, "Well, that's real enough, don't you think?" and she agreed. What I mean is that our relationship with step-children and grandchildren is established by us--not by how someone else defines it. Instead of worrying about what the grandchildren call her she can just BE a good grandmother. When she has the opportunity to visit, give the grandchildren plenty of positive attention. Then, it doesn't matter what they call her because it's all about love anyway.

Passive-aggressive Example 40 Husband's Unreasonable Expectations of ADD Wife

Question: My husband knows that I suffer from Attention Deficit Disorder (ADD} which means sometimes I'm not really in the moment when I am doing something. The way he pushes my buttons is to put something somewhere and leave it there knowing that I am working or cleaning in that particular area of the house and he does not say "I need you not to move or touch this thing right here." Then he becomes loud and aggressive when I move it and do not realize where I moved it to.

Response: First, the wife needs to be cautious in her assumption and interpretation of her husband's behavior and his intention. Although his behavior could be passive-aggressive (PA), it is also possible he is reacting out of frustration. He may not be as aware of her ADD all the time like she believes he should be. Therefore, let's look at this situation in three ways: 1) he is not being PA; 2) he is being PA; and 3) challenging her interpretation of the situation.

He is not being PA. Her husband may not be thinking about her ADD. Often, we think people are aware of something (because we've told them repeatedly). Yet, most people are responding to situations from their own perspective. In addition, ADD can be quite variable, and therefore, confusing to an outsider's perspective. What I mean is that the ADD symptoms of lack of focus and memory problems are often inconsistent--a person might be able to focus and remember in one situation and not another. Therefore, even though her husband knows she has ADD, he may not always have that in mind and interpret her behavior according to that fact. As a result, when he is reacting it is not due to PA but just frustration about his things being misplaced.

The reason it is important to think of the possibility of this not being PA behavior is because then the problem might be more readily resolved. In particular, they may need to discuss the problem when they are not in the heat of the moment and brainstorm possible solutions. Often, people believe that once they told somebody something once, the other person should always keep those instructions in mind. ADD or no ADD, people don't think that way. We need repeated reminders. If you WANT to make a change, do you tell yourself once and then you have made the change? Or do you need to keep reminding yourself? I find when I'm working with people to make changes, often the hardest thing is remembering. When I ask if they practiced their assignment, initially the response is often "I forgot." And this is with people who are fairly motivated to change. So, both the wife and the husband need to keep in mind that changing behavior requires repeated reminders. And these reminders can't be in anger because then all that is remembered is the anger and the argument. Instead, they need to brainstorm other possible solutions. For example, when the wife is cleaning she could put out a sign (similar to the "wet floor" signs put up in public places) to warn her husband that if he sets anything down it might be put away and forgotten. Or, the husband could put a post-it note on the things he doesn't want touched--if she needs to move them, she could indicate on the post-it note where the item is. In this way, they may solve the problem rather than having the repeated argument.

He is being PA. On the other hand, maybe the husband is PA and he takes delight in setting things down for his wife to misplace so that he can pounce on her and take his frustrations out on her. Notice, however, my description shows a very deliberate and well thought-out plan. If this is the situation, most likely the same behavior is occurring in other areas of their marriage.

PA behavior has a purpose. In this case, the purpose would be to escalate an argument so that he can feel better by releasing his anger while blaming her. By doing so, he doesn't have to take responsibility for his behavior. In this type of situation, as I have described elsewhere, it is important to not reward his behavior. The reward is the ability to take his frustrations out on her. To reduce the reward she needs to refrain from escalating the argument by removing herself from it as calmly as possible: "I will discuss this with you when you are calmer." Obviously, she may not be able to prevent the reward completely because he might feel satisfied with his initial blaming reaction or he might try to continue the argument. If that is the case, they may have more serious problems to address.

Challenging her interpretation. Finally, there may be some assumptions she is making that affect how she views the situation. By examining her own thinking, she may be better able to determine whether his behavior is likely to be PA or not.

Passive-aggressive Example 41 Back-stabbing Doctor

Question: A doctor I work with feels I am "too proud" and independent in my work. He dislikes my personality, and that's ok-- we don't have to be buddies. But he has taken to telling each new group of residents that there is no point discussing anything with me because I am overbearing. He tells them they should just avoid discussion and agree with me. When I present an assessment in rounds he covers his eyes and bows his head. After he leaves, if I need to speak to one of the residents about a patient having problems, I can see them bracing themselves as I approach or rolling their eyes even though we may have never yet spoken to each other! I am viewed as a competant and compassionate doctor by families and co-workers, but this treatment is distracting and disheartening. It is making it difficult to provide safe care, to the point that I have considered leaving my practice.

Response: Even if this situation isn't the same as what other readers might experience, I think it can be a good learning exercise to think more creatively about how to respond to passive-aggressive (PA) behavior. Sometimes people are too focused on their own hurt, anger, and resentment that they don't look at other possible solutions. As I've indicated numerous times, normal communication and problem-solving skills don't work with PA people. Therefore, you need to be more creative in the solutions. Sometimes this might mean you need to step outside your comfort zone and engage in a different way.

The doctor is employing classic back-stabbing passive-aggressive behavior. He rallies each new group of residents to his side by gossiping about his colleague and turning them against her. He then reinforces his prior statements with his nonverbal gestures of covering his eyes and bowing his head. Back-stabbing PA behavior is one of the more difficult PA situations to manage because most attempts to confront the behavior would lead to more of the same. If confronted, the doctor is rewarded for his behavior because he knows that he is successfully distressing his colleague while being favored by the residents. Most likely this is some sort of ego booster for him often used by less competent people to discredit those who are more competent.

Although there is a way to probably stop his PA behavior during rounds, it takes a high level of skill that most people don't have and it will not stop his talking behind her back. For instance, when he engages in the PA nonverbal behaviors, she could very sweetly say, "Doctor, when you cover your eyes and bow your head like that it makes me think you disagree--what do you think of my assessment?" However, this needs to be delivered with just the right tone and facial expression of innocence (without any hint of sarcasm) so it is difficult for many people to pull off. It can be an effective way, though, to get him to stop the nonverbals. And at the same time it makes her appear more open to discussion which refutes his private insinuations to the residents. At first he is likely to bluster that she is misinterpreting but if she calls him out every time he is likely to stop.

However, as I said, that is difficult to pull off. In this case, it may be necessary to get to the residents before he does. The good thing about this scenario is that his behavior is predictable and residents rotate in and out. Therefore, his behavior doesn't poison her relationships permanently because those residents will be gone. If she can focus on developing a good first impression with the residents when they first arrive then his back-stabbing will be less effective. Yes, this will take more effort and may be uncomfortable if it is not consistent with her personality style. But I don't think it is more effort or more uncomfortable than having to leave a successful practice. So what she can do is before the residents come on rotation she can meet with them individually or as a group for an informal welcome. For instance, she could take them to lunch and let them get to know her in an informal setting. In this way, she prevents their only impression of her being the other doctor's gossip. They are less likely to take his comments to heart as his statements are not consistent with their impression of her.

If she does this, she doesn't have to address anything with them about the other doctor but just have an enjoyable lunch. However, if she would like to counter-act his statements even more she could say something like: "I know I can get quite intense during rounds because I am so passionate about this work, but don't let that bother you. I still welcome other opinions so feel free to let me know what you think." A statement like this establishes a working relationship with the residents and negates his back-stabbing. In fact, the combination of these suggestions could make him look like a jerk without her ever saying a word about him!

Passive-aggressive Example 42
Why Does My Husband Want a "Reward" for Hurting Me?

Question: Best article on passive/aggressive. Wish I read this 27 years ago. Didn't know what I have been dealing with. Why does my husband want a "reward" of seeing me hurt, upset, put down? Is this sick behavior learned from watching his parents? Will he ever "want" to treat me nice? Or is he incapable? I just want a husband who loves me and acts like it. I have been telling him for years his behavior is emotionally abusive, but he cant seem to stop. Why? Why is his reward to see me unhappy?

Response: Great question! The concept of "reward" (as we psychologists use it) can be very confusing. It comes from the behavior modification literature referring to the idea that people increase behavior they are rewarded for and reduce behavior when they do not receive a reward (or are punished). The easiest way to think of this idea is to consider a child who is screaming and is being disruptive in a public place. The parent desperately wants to quiet the child so the parent gives the child a piece of candy. The child has just been "rewarded" for bad behavior. What does the child learn from this? The child learns that misbehaving has benefits. But that doesn't mean the child thinks through the process: "If I scream, I will get candy." Instead, it is what we call a learned behavior which is something that is done automatically. It's sort of like stopping at a red light--once you have learned to drive, you don't think "I need to stop" when you see a red light, you just automatically stop because your brain has learned to associate a red light with pressing the brake with your foot.

In the situation with your husband it doesn't mean that he is thinking "I will get a reward if I hurt you and cause you to be unhappy" but that he is engaging in an automatic behavior that probably has been rewarded in some way throughout his life. For example, let's say a spouse was raised in an emotionally abusive home and, as a result, tries to avoid uncomfortable emotions especially those that caused feelings of worthlessness and powerlessness as a child. One way of avoiding those emotions might be to deflect the blame on to another person. By doing so he is "rewarded" by not having to feel uncomfortable. However, this process is subconscious so he is not aware of what he is doing. In fact, in this example, it has to remain subconscious because to be aware of what he is doing he would have to feel the uncomfortable emotions he is avoiding.

This is why my article discusses trying to respond to passive-aggressive (PA) people by determining what the reward might be for their behavior and then not giving them the reward. Although some PA people may be aware of what they are doing, much of the time they are not which means you can't address the behavior directly. In fact, usually they are very well protected psychologically because the whole point is to not take responsibility for their behavior because that would cause them to feel bad about themselves (which is what they are avoiding).

However, to try to determine the reward for your husband means that instead of looking at it from your point of view you need to look at what he gets from the situation. His reward probably isn't seeing you unhappy, but when be behaves a certain way and you react, what is he able to avoid? Sometimes you may not be able to know the underlying cause of his behavior which is why one of the best ways to respond to PA people is to not react. You know your reaction is a reward in some way so by not reacting he doesn't get the reward. For instance, what if you don't get upset? What if you just smile, ignore his comment, and go about your day? He doesn't get the reward.

Does that mean his behavior will change? Probably not from just ignoring him because it has been ingrained over a lifetime. However, once you stop rewarding him for bad behavior, you could start rewarding him for good behavior (borrowing another concept from behavior modification). This works really well for someone who still has that scared child inside of him because of emotionally abusive parents (which you allude to in your comment about "watching his parents").

Let's go back to that example of the child getting a piece of candy for bad behavior. Most parents know that if you stop rewarding a child for throwing tantrums and try to ignore the behavior instead, the tantrums get worse initially. But after a time, the behavior might start to decrease. So, the idea then is to reward the good behavior. When the child doesn't throw a tantrum, you praise the child for being so well-behaved.

In a similar way, you could start watching for small signs of good behavior from your husband and reward those. Instead of pointing out his emotional abusiveness, you could comment about anything he says or does that you like. "You are so kind to make sure my oil is changed." "Give me a hug--your hugs make me feel good." "I know you're trying to give me helpful advice and I appreciate it." Like I said earlier, for people who are protecting themselves from feeling bad, rewarding good behavior can be a powerful motivator for change. However, just as the PA behavior is subconscious, the change is subconscious, too. Overtime, you may see increased good behavior because it feels good to be rewarded. But instead of being rewarded for bad behavior (through your reaction to his PA comments) he is rewarded for when he treats you better.

One last thing--you may have noticed I said to watch for "small signs" of good behavior. One reason for this is when a couple is in a PA pattern for a long time, there may not be many good behaviors to reward. So, in behavior modification we have a concept known as "successive approximations to the goal." What this means is that we start by rewarding any behavior that is even remotely in the direction that we want and then shape the behavior over time. For instance, if you want to teach a bird to peck a target, you can't wait for the bird to accidentally peck a target and then reward the bird because that will probably never happen. Instead, you have to shape its behavior. To do this, you could start rewarding the bird with a piece of food whenever it is in the side of the cage where the target is. Then, once it is spending more time on that side of the cage you could start rewarding it when it is the vicinity of the target. Then, once that occurs more frequently, you could reward it when it is touching the target. In this way you have shaped the bird to the point where it will touch the target more and eventually peck the target accidentally. When that occurs, you could begin only rewarding the bird whenever it pecks the target.

I know some people object to the idea that human behavior is so mechanistic. However, in a situation where a person is acting from subconscious learned behaviors, shaping their behavior can be quite an effective method.

Passive-aggressive Example 43 Deliberate Annoyances Followed by Denial

Question: I like to have an egg with a piece of toast and jelly for breakfast. This morning while cooking a couple eggs in my egg cooker I put a piece of bread in the toaster. After a while I thought my toast was taking more time than usual. I opened the toaster and found my toast almost burnt. Upon inspection, I saw the time had been turned up. She hadn't used that toaster for quite awhile. I have, so I know she must've turned it up. I didn't confront her because I have found out that's the reward she wants. When I react she gets to argue with me and first thing I know she's blaming me, turning the conversation towards me, telling me I'm getting senile or I'm crazy. Sometimes I almost believe her. It's enough to make you crazy. She's been doing this all our marriage and I just became aware of PA behavior recently. It's an every day occurance. If she gets mad at me, I start keeping an eye open for what she's going to do to get even. The things she does are not damaging, but are things I've asked her not to do. I get frustrated because I know she does it on purpose. If I confront her she says, "What did I do? I didn't do that. Your losing it!" If I say anything more, it becomes a loud argument and then she blames me for something totally different. I cannot outargue her.

Response: Fortunately, most PA behavior is not intentional but is due to either learning ineffective communication styles in childhood or to avoiding the discomfort of directly expressing anger. However, in this situation, assuming the accuracy of the interpretation based upon repeated instances of this behavior, the PA behavior is clearly intentional. In fact, it is classic revenge-seeking PA behavior with the purpose of not only expressing anger but retaliating and causing hurt. The person who engages in this behavior wants to cause the other person pain and not only not be responsible for it but to blame, escalate, and make their victim look like the "crazy" one. This allows the attacker to feel justified for raging.

Why does the person need to rage? The answer can vary from person to person. Generally, though, raging can be a release of pent-up emotions. Such a release and venting of emotions can feel good. Some people need the release due to another underlying problem such as depression. Temporarily they may get some relief from the depression when they rage. Other people may have what we refer to as "over-controlled" anger in which they allow minor annoyances to build up until they explode. However, raging about "you didn't close the cap on the toothpaste" only makes them look ridiculous so the PA behavior of creating and escalating conflict allows justification of the rage.

Unfortunately, this individual has little incentive for change. Confronting her only gives her the opportunity for escalation which gives her the desired release of being able to yell at him and tell him that he is crazy. In such a way, she can deny any responsibility and ignore her own problems. Probably the most the husband can do is to keep his sanity by recognizing the PA behavior and understanding that it is not him. By not engaging with her he can prevent the blame and escalation part of the revenge strategy. By doing so he prevents her from being able to justify her anger, attack him further, and get the release she desires.

My concern in a revenge-seeking type of situation is that if she is denied the powerful release he may need to be prepared for an escalation of tactics. With this type of person, if she is not satisfied she may escalate from minor annoyances to more damaging behavior. If this occurs, it may be necessary to allow her a little release just to keep her in check. I know this isn't the best way to handle the situation, but sometimes options are limited. Or, he may try some way to deflect the problem early on before she engages in the retaliatory PA behavior. For instance, he says "if she gets mad at me I start keeping an eye open for what she's going to do to get even." This statement indicates he knows that she is mad at him and he can predict the PA response. Maybe it is possible to deal with her anger at that point.

From a psychological viewpoint, I imagine in her mind that when he does things that annoy her she believes he is deliberately hurting her. The reason I say this is because people frequently use the defense mechanism of projection which is denying their own behavior while accusing others of the same behavior: a liar believes everyone lies, a rude person accuses everyone of being rude. So, in this case, she deliberately hurts him which is likely to mean that she believes that he intentionally hurts her.

I understand that she should be more responsible for her behavior and she should be the one to change. However, that is not the reality in this situation. She is a child acting out her anger. And as such, she needs to learn to express her anger more appropriately. Just as a parent puts words to a child's anger to teach a child how to express the anger appropriately, by putting words to his wife's anger, he might help her to be able to express herself without needing to seek revenge. Perhaps, when he knows she is angry, if he helps her put words to her anger and helps her resolve it, she wouldn't have a need for the revenge behavior: "I know you are angry with me and I sincerely don't want to cause you pain--what is it that you would like from me?" or "I didn't mean to hurt you. How can we make this better?" or "I know I can be annoying--what is it that's bothering you?" Although I know this is a long shot, by doing so, he may derail some of the PA behavior before it starts.

Passive-aggressive Example 44
What Do I Do When I am Ignored Most of the Time?

Question: My boyfriend moved into my home with me 3 years ago. His two boys, now 17 and 20, spend one overnight a week and a couple of hours mid-week with us. They told their dad before he moved in that they would rather he keep his own apartment so they could visit with just him. We went ahead with co-habitation and things quickly soured.

99% of the time the boys speak to me only when spoken to, usually in one word or one sentence replies. Sometimes they say hello to me and sometimes not. Most of the time, I try to engage them but I'm aware that I generalize at times, and as a result, don't engage beyond hello and goodbye because "It will have the same negative outcome." However, I recognize the irrationality of this and usually attempt to start afresh.

They rarely eat any foods I prepare, opting for frozen/canned. We rarely go anywhere together as a group, usually because I'm not invited. The older boy rarely speaks to anyone. The younger one is much more talkative with others. Their dad has spoken to them regarding politeness, greetings, ad nauseam. I've spoken to the younger boy twice about how it makes me feel sad when he doesn't talk to me or say hello and goodbye. The younger one was taken to a therapy session or two and refused to go back.

I argue with their dad about it, sometimes giving him ultimatums and putting him in a no-win situation.

I hope you can assist as I admire you and the enlightening, comprehensive website you've created. It is helping me tremendously as I read, listen, write and practice.

I read a suggestion in one of the PA articles that it may be helpful to regularly and often tell the persons how their behavior makes you feel in a calm, collected way. For example, maybe I could say, "S--- and R----, it hurts my feelings when I'm not included in conversations." And say it every visit they don't talk to me.

What can I do differently?

Response: My first suggestion would be to work on not taking this personally. I know that can be difficult when it feels so personal. But keep in mind that you are talking about boys between the ages of 14 (when you first met) to 20. I used to say when we had two 16-year-old boys in our home at the same time, "They should round up all the 16-year-old boys and put them on another planet!" In other words, this is a difficult time for many parents so it is really not about you. The good thing, though, this behavior changes as they grow up. I've seen young men who acted this way at 20 who seem like they were replaced by a body snatcher at age 28--completely different!

Also, it is particularly difficult to get boys this age to behave the way you want. So their dad probably doesn't have much control over their behavior especially since he hasn't had full custody of them. One thing he might be able to try that I found effective and many of my clients have as well is a natural consequence approach (read my PsychNote: Natural Consequences for Children). However, beyond that, he really can't control the behavior.

In general, letting an unintentional PA person know when they hurt you is a good idea because it confronts them with their behavior. However, for this to be effective they have to care at some level. I doubt that boys this age really care whether they are hurting your feelings. So in this situation I think confronting the behavior will only make them more sullen and withdrawn from you.

Instead, if you can refrain from taking it personally and from looking for a positive outcome, it may be better to just pretend the behavior doesn't exist. In other words, be pleasant, talk to them, ask your boyfriend to include you in activities, but otherwise ignore this behavior. And one day you might be like many parents who are suddenly shocked when they realize their young adult child is talking to them.

A final note--be cautious about your own withdrawal. Otherwise, you may also be seen as engaging in PA withdrawal to express your frustration. I realize it is unintentional but it may not be viewed that way by the recipients.

Passive-aggressive Example 45 Problems with Adult Child Living at Home

Question: Our 19-year-old daughter has always been a handful. She suffers from generalized anxiety disorder and anorexia diagnosed at age 13. She is in college but will not live on campus and refused to drive until age 18. Now she leaves our home at 8:AM every day but will not return home until past midnight. She will not contribute to our home, leaves filth everywhere she goes. She is dating two young men who look as though they have crawled out from under a rock. She is intelligent and beautiful. When confronted about her filth and lack of contribution at home she claims her stress level is off the charts. Her therapist claims she is a normal latent teen due to her earlier issues. She reals me in with advice about juggling her beaus or classes but lashes out at me when I advise her to slow down or ask her to clean her filth. I have become resentful of her and she of me. We got into an altercation where she pushed, shoved, and hit me. I hit her back to get her off of me. Then she left home claiming she was afraid to come back. Her father took her side saying I must have provoked her when all I asked her to do is clean her room. She is back home but nothing has changed except now I am dealing with her verbal disrespect.

Example: **Me** - "Good morning, last night you left used sanitary products exposed in the downstairs bathroom. Will you take care of that immediately?"

Her - "Isn't it so nice to be greeted with griping and complaining first thing in the morning."

Me- "Seriously? Go clean that up--no one wants to see it."

Her - "I will if I get a chance. You are stressing me out."

Me - "You need to be stressed out, clean your mess up now."

Her - "I am late for class." Door slams, car drives off, mess stays.

Me -???

Response: I dealt with a very similar situation with a client who had an adult daughter living at home and a husband taking the daughter's side. This requires a bit of finesse and is a three-step process. It is probably best for you to see a cognitive-behavioral therapist to help with implementing these steps. You may not like what I have to say but keep in mind as your read this that I'm not taking her side but I'm trying to give you a blueprint for a realistic way of changing a difficult situation.

First, it is necessary for you to recognize that you can't change another person. You can only change yourself. The goal here, I assume, is to have a more tolerable living condition. At the moment your focus is on what she should do to make it more tolerable for you. Even though you are not using the word "should" I see it implied throughout your description: "She should get herself together", "She should make better choices in her relationships", "She should be more respectful", "She should at least contribute at home and clean her room." Such "shoulds" are demands and expectations for her to change. But as I said, you can't change her. Only by changing yourself do you have the opportunity to change a situation. Why is that? Because every family is a system that operates together. If you change any part of that system, the other parts have to change in response, for better or worse. But the only part of that system you have control over is yourself. So that is the only part you can change. However, if you plan a change carefully, you can potentially have a positive impact.

Am I saying that the problem is all you and she is not contributing to it? No--I am saying that people typically change only when their behavior causes them a problem. In this situation her behavior is causing you a problem, not her. So she doesn't have any incentive to change. The goal, then, is that by taking these steps and changing your behavior you can give her a greater incentive for change.

The second step is to recognize her mental illness and the struggles she has to overcome so that you can focus on more positive interactions. Again, from your statements there is an implied blame for her mental illness. "She...will not live on campus and refused to drive until age 18" does not recognize her anxiety about those things. Instead, you say it as if she should be able to do these things and just doesn't want to.

From what I am hearing is that your relationship has devolved into attacking her with criticism and her defending herself by attacking back. As I have written elsewhere, this pattern can change by you choosing to focus on positive qualities and behavior. This does not mean you can't ever criticize but it is best to keep criticism to a ratio of five positives to every criticism--since your situation has deteriorated so much, a ratio of ten positives to every negative may be better. Criticism can better be heard in the context of an overall positive relationship. And the positives can't be general as in "You are intelligent" or a backhanded compliment as in "You are so beautiful. I'm sure you could find better men to date." Praise needs to be very specific. You might say to me "She doesn't do anything that is positive! How can I possibly say positive things to her?" And that is the challenge. By committing yourself to having five positive interactions for every negative one it forces you to look for the positives. It also tends to reduce the criticisms because you know you will have to make up for it with five positive interactions.

Finally, you can begin to set consequences for her behavior. I know it will be tempting to start with this step but don't do this without the other steps first or it will backfire on you! And step two may take quite awhile before you start noticing positive changes. Also, this step may not be necessary because she might respond to the improved quality of your relationship.

Consequences for adult children living at home can be very difficult especially when you don't have the support of your spouse. So you have to determine what you actually have control of. You don't have control of her nor do you have control of your husband. You only have control of what you do. For instance, you can close the door to her room because you don't have control over her cleaning her room. If she leaves things laying around the house, put them in a box (yes, including the used sanitary products), and put it in front of her door. Don't explain or criticize. This may seem to be passive-aggressive retaliation which is why it is important that it be done without anger and by first establishing a more positive atmosphere. I had one mother whose daughter wouldn't clean up her dishes so the mother started putting the dishes in the daughter's doorway without saying a word--eventually, the daughter started cleaning up her dishes.

Another type of consequence is not doing things that you would normally do for her. For instance, if she makes a request of you, check internally with yourself and see how you feel about her behavior that day. If it has been positive, grant her request (if reasonable), otherwise don't. It is important to do this without explanation and to not carry your resentment over from previous days. If she asks "why not?" tell her calmly "I don't like how you treated me today and just don't feel like it."

Also, stop giving advice. That can be a passive-aggressive trap. Instead, just listen to her and ask what she thinks. In other words, just help her think it through. For instance, when she tells you what she thinks, ask (without any sarcasm) "How do you think that will help?" or "If you do that, what do you expect will occur?"

So, if you take these steps and make these changes, what incentive is there for her to change? One reason is that people with mental illness often have low self-esteem. You are an important influence in her life and by increasing the positive interactions you are likely to increase her positive feelings for herself and her desire to have a better relationship with you. Another incentive for change is the consequences. When her behavior affects her more than you, then she may change the behavior.

Passive-aggressive Example 46 Passive Control as a Form of Passive-Aggression

Question: I have a 20-year-old daughter. She is an amazing young woman, going to college, working, and doing mission work twice a year in third world countries. I pay for her college, her housing, car and insurance. Her job affords her to buy food, fuel, and spending money. For the most part, we have a good relationship, but I see it declining. Much like described in this article, I will have a discussion with her trying to be upbeat but always feeling like I'm walking on eggshells. Just tonight, I called her and in the middle of the discussion, she yells the F-word. She knows I don't like cussing, so I respond by saying maybe I should call her back later. She complains and acts very callous towards me. I no longer say anything about her behavior. When I have responded with anything similar to the recommended "Maybe I am but I don't like it when you treat me this way", her normal response is that I'm being over-sensitive. I have started creating a distance between us, but also want to continue to provide love and support to her.

Response: I have a couple reactions to this very common scenario and I think they're interrelated. My first reaction is that this mother may be engaging in subtle advice-giving when it is not desired. So in this case the PA behavior may be unintentional passive control on the mother's part. I know I'm reading into this situation so I will discuss what I have commonly seen in my practice.

My second reaction is that this is part of navigating the separation-individuation stage of development. Let's talk about that first since a successful outcome of that stage sets the tone for the future mother-daughter relationship.

The normal process of development that occurs in late adolescence and early adulthood is identity development. Many parents interfere with this process because it feels like their relationship is "declining" as this woman describes. However, that is not necessarily the case. She describes her daughter as "amazing" and that they have a good relationship. I think especially in the case of parents who have good relationships with their adolescent children, they are surprised at the changes in the relationship and will tend to interfere with this process in subtle ways because they see it as a bad thing. Instead, they need to accept it as necessary for proper development.

What is separation-individuation and identity development? In a nutshell, it is the process of identifying oneself as a separate entity from the parent. It is making one's own decisions, taking pleasure in successful outcomes and owning failures. That might sound great but the process can be difficult. The process means questioning and rejecting values and beliefs that have been taught and replacing them with chosen ones. Some of these may be similar or the same to parental values and some may not.

What is the parent's job during this process? The parent needs to recognize her job of raising her child is finished and the time is coming to form a new adult relationship with the child. This is a time of change and can be quite difficult especially when the parent expects the relationship to remain the same or smoothly transition. During this time many parents feel that the relationship is deteriorating when, instead, it is transforming. Creating distance during this process is normal and often necessary as too much closeness can interfere with identity development.

To help with this transformation some things to examine:

1) **Worry**. This mother is worrying about their relationship and not being as involved in her daughter's life. This is a time to learn to let go of the worry even though it has been her job as a mother to worry. This is a time, instead, when she can focus on trusting that she has taught her daughter well.

2) **Subtle criticism**. "Don't you think...?" "Are you sure...?" "It might be a good idea to ...."

Would you say these things to a friend who hadn't asked for advice? An adult relationship with a child means to stop giving unsolicited advice. When a parent does so they are undermining a child's confidence and the child is likely to react with anger. "Love and support" means to be there when the adult child desires it but not to be overly involved otherwise. 3) Focus. If the daughter is reacting with anger most likely the mother is focused on the daughter. If the mother was talking about her own day or her interests, it is doubtful the daughter would yell "the F-word" in the middle of the conversation. So it is also time for the mother to begin to focus on herself. This prevents the daughter from feeling like her life is being dissected.

I would suggest for further information to read the chapter: Are You Passive-Aggressive and Want to Change? It can provide guidance for those who are unintentionally PA because of their concern, worry, or over-involvement.

Passive-aggressive Example 47 Getting in the Middle of Passive-Aggression

Question: Sister-in-law makes comment to brother's wife that she should be more receptive to his dreams after working hard all his life and as money is not a problem. Wife responds by telling husband that his sister is telling everyone she is controlling and "your sister hates me." She also tells him that his sister makes sure he's not around when she goes off on her with hurtful non-specific insults. The brother believes all the lies told to him and blocks his sister from his life. The sister truly loves her brother and was trying to help with his dreams. She wishes to resolve the matter with her brother and his wife together but doesn't know how to do that with the PA wife without calling her a liar. This occurred during a period when the sister had lost a child and the brother continued to call her a liar during her depression and block her from contact. The sister is worried to call the PA wife out because it may end the relationship forever. She is hurting and needs help to expose the PA lies without totally ruining the relationship or even knowing if it's worth saving.

Response: The sister indicates she wants to salvage this relationship with her brother and sister-in-law. Assuming that is sincere, it is necessary for her to examine her own behavior as well. If she is willing to do so, it is possible for the relationship to be saved (of course, it also depends on the brother and his wife's willingness). A good starting point can be reading the chapter Are You Passive-Aggressive and Want to Change? In that article I state "Those who are passive-aggressive (PA) and want to change are usually unintentionally PA. In other words, they are not trying to maliciously cause problems for others..." which is the basis for the rest of my response to this situation.

This scenario appears to be two passive-aggressive (PA) women who have put the brother/husband in the middle of a feud. The reason I say that is because the sister first used a "should" on the wife and then responded with innocence when the wife became angry. In addition, she wants to "call the PA wife out" and "expose the PA lies." This is a PA desire, not a desire to save the relationship. In other words, she wants to vindicate her behavior and make the sister-in-law out to be a liar. Remember, the root of PA behavior is anger that is expressed in a passive way. If the sister approaches this situation with the desire to expose the wife's lies while indicating she wants to "resolve the matter" she is disguising her anger as an attempt to resolve the problem and is likely to proclaim innocence when the attempt implodes.

Certainly, the brother and his wife are engaging in PA behavior as well -- withdrawal and backstabbing. However, they are not asking how to solve the situation so their behavior can't be dealt with in this response. But for the sister's sake, let's look at their behavior by giving them the benefit of the doubt and assume they are also engaging in unintentional PA behavior because they don't have the skills to know how to respond in a better way. For instance, the wife is angry at the sister but instead of expressing her anger directly, she complains to her husband and expects him to resolve it. The husband feels put in the middle of the situation and just wants out so he withdraws from the relationship with his sister.

So, if the sister truly wants to save this relationship, she needs to accept their limitations as well as her own and recognize that all of them have poor conflict resolution skills but are not maliciously trying to hurt one another. By having empathy for them and for herself she can then approach this situation in a different way.

And how would that be? Apologize. Pure and simple. Do not blame them. Do not focus on the wife's or the brother's behavior. Recognize that the initial "should" is blaming and controlling PA and then apologize for it: "I realize that I was wrong in trying to tell you how to live your lives. I really want us to be close again. Please forgive me." Period.

About the Author

Dr. Monica Frank, a clinical psychologist who has provided services to individuals with anxiety, depressive, and stress-related disorders for over 25 years in St. Louis, Missouri, USA, is the founder of Excel At Life, LLC. Previously, Dr. Frank developed and operated Behavioral Consultants, P.C., an intensive day treatment program for severe anxiety disorders in addition to an outpatient clinical practice.

Her current work through Excel At Life focuses on providing the public with tools and materials from cognitive-behavioral therapy (CBT) which can aid in the pursuit of personal growth as well as an adjunct to treatment for anxiety, depression, and other disorders. She draws on her clinical experience, scientific research, and training in the martial arts to create these tools and other materials which include articles, audios, and Android apps.

In addition to her Ph.D. in clinical psychology from St. Louis University she has extensive graduate level coursework from Southern Illinois University-Edwardsville in the area of sport psychology. Her undergraduate degree was from the University of Missouri-St. Louis.

Dr. Frank's strong interest in Eastern philosophies and Buddhist psychology has led her to train in various forms of Tai Chi/Qi Gong as well as other mindfulness methods for over 15 years. She is a third degree black belt in American Kenpo and continues her involvement in martial arts at the Martial Arts Center.

Available Books

The Porcupine Effect: Pushing Others Away When You Want to Connect

Happy Habits: 50 Suggestions

Stop Panic and Anxiety: 50 Tools

The Cognitive Diary Method to Changing Your Life

The Mindful Attitude: Understanding Mindfulness and the Steps to Developing Emotional Tolerance

Printed in Great Britain
by Amazon

33915856R00121